Complete Science

With Fun Experiments, Cool Science Facts and Trivia Questions

Grade **6**

William Young

Printed in China

ISBN: 978-1-897457-78-8

Table of Contents

Section 1

Understanding Life Systems

Students will learn about biodiversity and investigate the impacts of environmental conditions and human activities on biodiversity. They will be introduced to the five kingdoms of living things and classify vertebrates into the five groups. The characteristics of some biomes, and their biotic and abiotic elements will also be discussed. Students will also recognize that there is diversity within a species and that living things depend on one another for many reasons.

ISBN: 978 1 897457 78 8

Section 2

Understanding Structures and Mechanisms

Students will study the properties of air and recognize how these properties are applied in their daily lives. They will investigate the four forces of flight – thrust, drag, lift, and gravity – and learn how aircraft create different movements in the air with these forces. Moreover, they will learn about airfoils and the Bernoulli's principle, and use the principle to explain how lift happens. They will compare the flight mechanisms in some living things with human-made flying machines.

Table of
Contents

Section 3

Understanding Matter and Energy

Students will learn about current electricity and static electricity and the differences between them. They will be introduced to simple circuits and their main components. The differences between open and closed circuits, and series and parallel circuits, will also be examined. Students will study insulators and conductors, as well as the purpose of using each. In addition, they will learn how electrical energy can be transformed from or into other forms of energy. They will realize the impacts of electricity and know how to reduce the use of electricity.

ISBN: 978-1-897457-78-8

Section 4

Understanding Earth and Space Systems

Students will identify the bodies in the solar system and know that some bodies emit light while others reflect light. They will recognize that different bodies are made up of different substances and have different orbital paths. They will also learn the effects of the relative positions of the Earth, the moon, and the sun. In addition, students will appreciate how technology helps humans meet their basic biological needs in space and how space exploration affects our society.

ISBN: 978-1-897457-78-8

ISBN: 978 1 897 57 78 8

Section 1

Understanding Life Systems

ISBN: 978-1-897457-78-8

1 Biodiversity

Biodiversity is the variety of living things on Earth. Scientists have named about 1.5 million different kinds of plants and animals, but they estimate that there are another million waiting to be discovered and named. In this unit, you will learn to recognize biodiversity and see how it occurs in the world.

After completing this unit, you will

- understand what biodiversity is.
- know that environmental conditions affect biodiversity.
- understand that new species are constantly being discovered.

Vocabulary

biological: relating to living things

diversity: variety, differences

diversity

ISBN: 978-1-897457-78-8

Diversity of life is important in the lives of all living things. Diversity in other areas may be important or just plain interesting. Look at the different examples of diversity we may have in our lives.

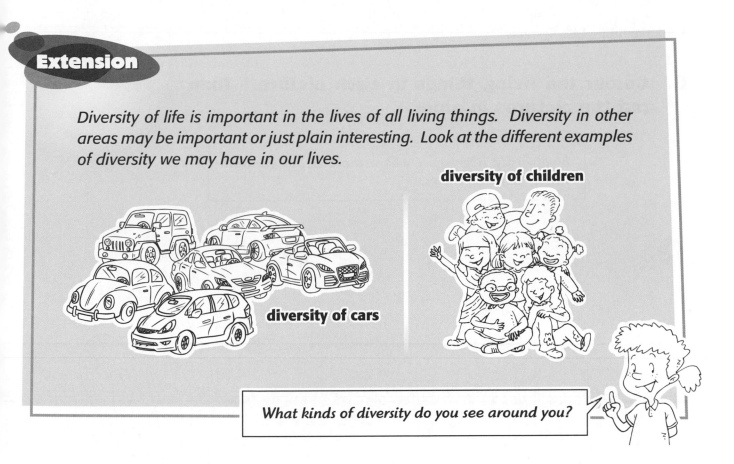

diversity of children

diversity of cars

What kinds of diversity do you see around you?

A. Fill in the missing letters. Then check the correct answers.

Biodiversity = _ _ _ _ logical ➕ d_ _ v _ _ _ s _ _ ty

1. Biodiversity means

   (A) the variety of living things.

   (B) one kind of living thing.

   (C) the variety of non-living things.

Biodiversity is two words joined together.

2. Biodiversity is found

   (A) on Earth.

   (B) in healthy forests.

   (C) in both of the above.

B. Colour the living things in each picture. Then put the pictures in order.

> *Biodiversity is greatest where there is the greatest variety of living things.*

From the greatest biodiversity to the least: _____

C. Find the things that show biodiversity. Write the letters.

Evidence of Biodiversity:

1. something represented in art _____

2. something to eat _____

3. something from a seed _____

4. something to drink _____

5. something to hear _____

6. something that adds nutrients to the soil _____

7. something that does work underground _____

8. something that an animal calls home _____

9. something that a dog likes _____

10. something that makes a pet scratch _____

ISBN: 978-1-897457-78-8

D. Read the passage. Complete the information on the new species discovered in 2008.

Thousands of new plant and animal species are discovered each year, and each year, the International Institute for Species Exploration at Arizona State University lists the top 10. Here are five from 2008's Top 10 List:

Please Welcome Some **New Species**

Barbados threadsnake
- found in Barbados, a country in the Caribbean
- world's smallest snake; about 10 centimetres long

Tahina palm
- huge species of palm tree found in Madagascar, a country in Africa
- self-destructing; they use so many of their nutrients to produce flowers that they die within months of flowering

Satomi's pygmy seahorse
- smallest known seahorse; 13.8 millimetres long
- found in waters off an island in Indonesia, a country in Southeast Asia

Charrier coffee
- first known naturally caffeine-free coffee species
- found in Cameroon, a country in Africa

Microbacterium hatanonis
- a species of bacterium found living in hairspray
- able to live in extreme environments
- discovered by Japanese scientists

ISBN: 978-1-897457-78-8

New Species Discovered in 2008

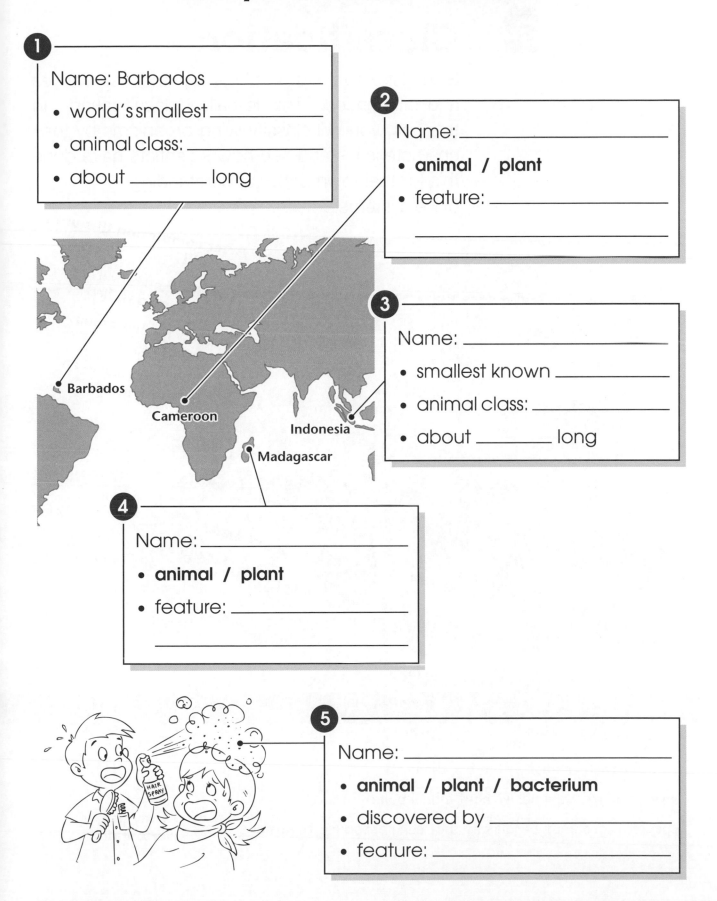

1

Name: Barbados _____

- world's smallest _____
- animal class: _____
- about _____ long

2

Name: _____

- **animal / plant**
- feature: _____
_____

3

Name: _____

- smallest known _____
- animal class: _____
- about _____ long

4

Name: _____

- **animal / plant**
- feature: _____
_____

5

Name: _____

- **animal / plant / bacterium**
- discovered by _____
- feature: _____

Barbados

Cameroon

Indonesia

Madagascar

2 Classification

Scientists sort living things by their similarities and differences. This is called classification. In this unit, you will classify living organisms by their characteristics and see how scientists have done this for their own better understanding of life systems.

After completing this unit, you will

- understand how living things are classified.
- know the five groups of vertebrates.
- know what makes an animal an insect.

vertebrates

invertebrates

Vocabulary

vertebrate: animal with a backbone

invertebrate: animal without a backbone

species: group of organisms that can reproduce together

backbone

X-ray fish
(vertebrate)

ISBN: 978-1-897457-78-8

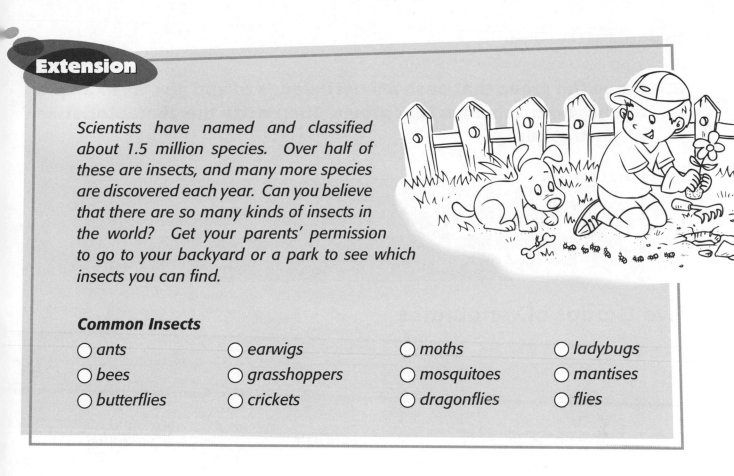

Scientists have named and classified about 1.5 million species. Over half of these are insects, and many more species are discovered each year. Can you believe that there are so many kinds of insects in the world? Get your parents' permission to go to your backyard or a park to see which insects you can find.

Common Insects

- ○ ants
- ○ bees
- ○ butterflies
- ○ earwigs
- ○ grasshoppers
- ○ crickets
- ○ moths
- ○ mosquitoes
- ○ dragonflies
- ○ ladybugs
- ○ mantises
- ○ flies

A. Complete the chart with the words in bold in the paragraph.

*All living things are divided into five kingdoms: **animals**, **plants**, **monerans**, **protists**, and **fungi**. The animal kingdom is divided into those with a backbone (**vertebrates**) and those without a backbone (**invertebrates**). Of the vertebrates, humans fit into one of five groups: **mammals**.*

Five Kingdoms of Life

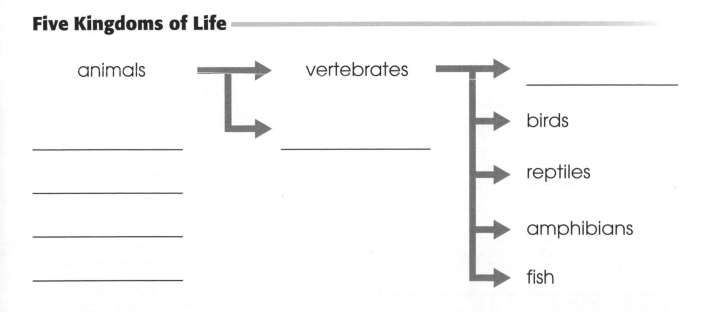

B. Name the group that each animal belongs to and give an example of one more animal in that group. Then write the characteristics of each group.

Characteristics

fins   feathers   moist skin   hair or fur

lay eggs on land   warm-blooded   lay eggs in water

nurse young   wings   cold-blooded   scales

Five Groups of Vertebrates

1. B_____

blue jay

e.g. _____

• characteristics

_____

_____

_____

_____

2. F_____

goldfish

e.g. _____

• characteristics

_____

_____

_____

_____

3. R_____

snake

e.g. _____

• characteristics

_____

_____

_____

4. A_____

salamander

e.g. _____

• characteristics

_____

_____

_____

5. M_____

dog

e.g. _____

• characteristics

_____

_____

_____

ISBN: 978-1-897457-78-8

C. Look at the body of an insect. Then fill in the blanks.

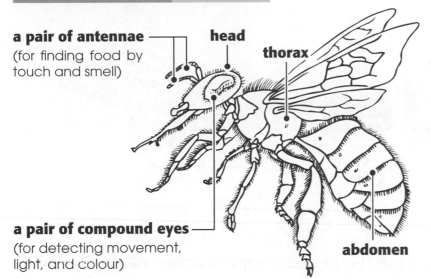

Invertebrates: **Insects**

a pair of antennae
(for finding food by
touch and smell)

head

thorax

a pair of compound eyes
(for detecting movement,
light, and colour)

abdomen

- Insects have no backbones, but are covered by an exoskeleton that is light and strong to keep out germs and provide protection against predators.

- Many insects have one or more pairs of wings.

Information about Insects

- are 1._____
  <u>invertebrates/vertebrates</u>

- are covered by a protective skeleton called an 2._____ , which is light and 3._____

- have 4._____ body segments – a 5._____ , 6._____ , and 7._____

- have a pair of 8._____ eyes to detect movement

- have a pair of 9._____ to find food

- have three pairs of 10._____ , for a total of 11._____ legs, to sense the world

- have one or more pairs of 12._____

D. Read the passage. Then complete the beetle fact sheet.

Beetles:
Big and Small

Beetles are a group of insects with the largest known number of species in the world. All beetle species have chewing mouthparts and well-developed antennae, and are characterized by a particularly hard exoskeleton and by protective outer non-flying wings that cover the flying wings (though not all beetles can fly). There are over 350 000 known species of beetles, and they come in many sizes.

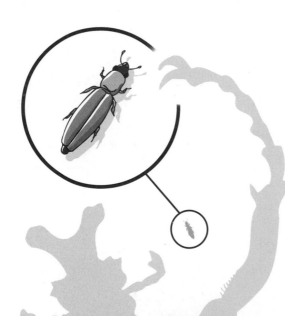

By weight, the world's biggest beetle is the Goliath Beetle. It reaches lengths of up to 11 centimetres and weighs up to 100 grams. Found in the tropical forests of Africa, it eats tree sap, fruit, dead plant material, and dung. Its colouring is usually a combination of brown, white, and black.

The world's smallest group of beetles are the Nanosellini. Their average length is less than 1 millimetre. These feather-winged beetles are found all over the world living on or in fungi. They eat fungal spores.

ISBN: 978-1-897457-78-8

Beetle Facts

- a group of <u>1.   </u>

insects/mammals/reptiles

- have the <u>2.   </u> known number of species in the world

smallest/largest

- have chewing <u>3.   </u>

- have a pair of well-developed <u>4.   </u>

- have a particularly hard <u>5.   </u>

- have protective outer <u>6.   </u> that cover the flying wings

7.

The biggest beetle : _____

Length : up to _____

Weight : up to _____

Habitat : _____

Diet : _____

Colour : _____

8.

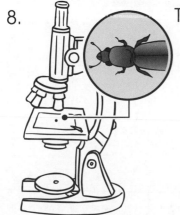

The smallest beetle : _____

Length : less than _____

Habitat : _____

Diet : _____

ISBN: 978-1-897457-78-8

3 Biodiversity and Communities

Biodiversity is found within communities. Within a species, diversity in genes can cause differences in appearance and behaviour. In this unit, you will learn that different ecosystems are a type of biodiversity, and that they support variety within a species, as well as differences among species.

Biome: Tropical Rainforest

After completing this unit, you will

- know the characteristics of some of the Earth's biomes.
- know the difference between biotic and abiotic elements.
- understand that there is diversity within a species.

Vocabulary

biome: a large natural area and the life it supports

biotic: living

abiotic: non-living

predator: animal that preys on another animal

permafrost: permanently frozen layer of ground below the ground's surface

predator

prey

ISBN: 978-1-897457-78-8

There is a balance of wildlife that human communities can and should support. For example, sharing our urban spaces with native plants and animals can make our cities healthier and our lives richer. Many urban areas have trees along streets, parks, and both natural and residential areas.

Look at the trees in your neighbourhood. See how they provide shelter for animals and soften the harsh texture of concrete buildings.

Look! A bird is flying from its nest!

A. Draw lines to match the biomes on Earth with the correct descriptions.

A biome is a large natural area where certain types of plants grow and certain types of animals feed on those plants.

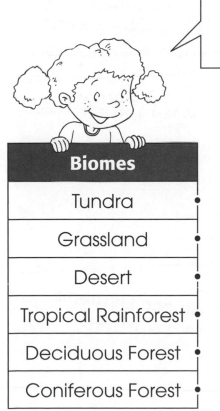

Biomes
Tundra
Grassland
Desert
Tropical Rainforest
Deciduous Forest
Coniferous Forest

- very little rainfall; cacti, lizards, and nocturnal animals

- fertile earth; grazing animals and their predators

- ice and permafrost; small plants and caribou

- trees that lose leaves in the winter; deer and songbirds

- warm temperatures, wet; many different species

- cool weather supporting evergreen trees; spruce and pine trees, beavers, and moose

ISBN: 978-1-897457-78-8

B. Look at the pictures of the two ecosystems. List the biotic and abiotic elements in each.

1.

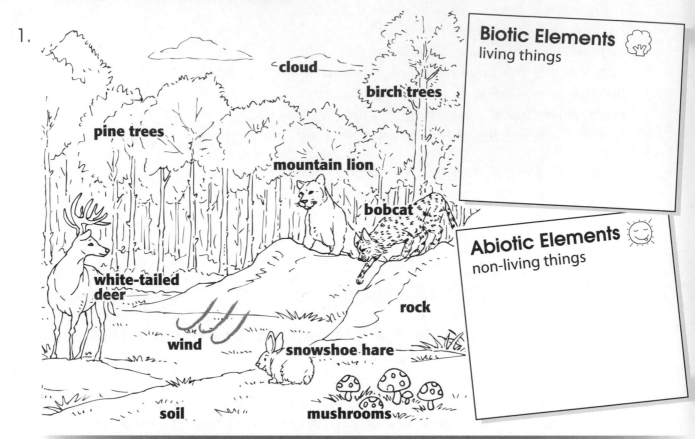

Biotic Elements 🌳
living things

Abiotic Elements ☺
non-living things

Labels in image: cloud, birch trees, pine trees, mountain lion, bobcat, white-tailed deer, rock, wind, snowshoe hare, soil, mushrooms

2.

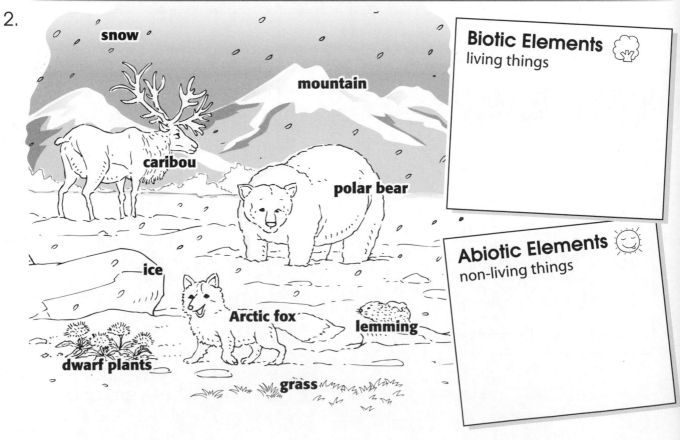

Biotic Elements 🌳
living things

Abiotic Elements ☺
non-living things

Labels in image: snow, mountain, caribou, polar bear, ice, Arctic fox, lemming, dwarf plants, grass

ISBN: 978-1-897457-78-8

C. Fill in the blanks with the given words. Colour the apples. Then answer the questions.

alike	diversity
genes	taste	cook

Genetic diversity is the diversity of 1._____ within a species. Even within a species, no two individuals are exactly 2._____ .

3._____ in apple trees is good because some varieties thrive in certain areas, while other varieties do not. We can also choose varieties of apples according to our 4._____ , and whether we want to eat them fresh or 5._____ them.

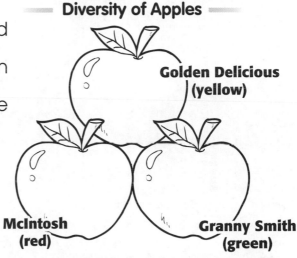

Diversity of Apples

Golden Delicious (yellow)

McIntosh (red)

Granny Smith (green)

6. Write about the differences and similarities in appearance of the two dogs below.

German Shepherd   **Poodle**

Differences: _____

_____

Similarities: _____

_____

7. Of these two kinds of dogs, which would you prefer to have? Explain your choice.

_____

_____

D. Read the passage. Then answer the questions.

Terrestrial Biomes
in Canada

There are six major terrestrial biomes in Canada: the **Temperate Rainforest**, found along the coast of British Columbia; the **Mountain Biome**, found in southern British Columbia and Alberta; the **Grassland**, found mostly in southern Alberta; three others are described below.

The **Tundra** is Canada's northernmost, coldest, driest, and least biologically diverse biome. There are no trees, but hardy grasses and shrubs grow. Animals include caribou and Arctic foxes.

The **Temperate Deciduous Forest** is Canada's most biologically diverse biome. Covering southeastern Canada, it is characterized by hot summers, cold winters, and rainfall of up to 150 cm each year. Deciduous trees like oak and maple dominate and animals include wolves, bobcats, and deer.

The **Boreal Forest** is a biome south of the tundra dominated by conifers like pine and spruce. Winters are cold and snowy, and up to 100 cm of precipitation falls each year. Animals include moose, bears, and deer.

ISBN: 978-1-897457-78-8

1. List the six major terrestrial biomes in Canada and their locations.

Six Major Terrestrial Biomes in Canada

- _____ ; _____
- _____ ; _____
- _____ ; _____
- _____ ; _____
- _____ ; _____
- _____ ; _____

2. Identify the biomes. Then complete the descriptions.

a. _____

   weather: cold and snowy in winter

   precipitation: up to _____ every

   year

   plants: _____ trees, e.g. pine

   animals: e.g. moose, _____ ,

   and _____

b. _____

   weather: hot summers, cold winters

   diversity: _____

   plants: _____ trees,

   e.g. _____

   animals: e.g. _____

   and _____

c. _____

   weather: extremely cold and dry

   diversity: least

   plants:

   e.g. _____

   _____

   animals:

   e.g.

   Arctic fox

   and _____

ISBN: 978-1-897457-78-8

Experiment

Introduction

> Humans need food, water, and warmth to grow. I need warmth, lots of sunlight, and just a bit of water to grow. Do other living things need specific conditions from their environments in order to grow?

Hypothesis

Living things need specific conditions to grow well.

Materials

- **3 sealable sandwich bags**
- **3 slices of bread from the same loaf**
- **a marker**
- **water**
- **an old towel**

Steps

1. Use the marker to number the bags from 1 to 3 and write the date on each one.

2. Splash a bit of water on your bread slices and place one in each bag. Seal the bags.

> *Make sure the bags are sealed and do not open them throughout the experiment.*

ISBN: 978-1-897457-78-8

3. Place bag 1 in the fridge, bag 2 in a cupboard, and bag 3 on a windowsill.

4. Bags 1 and 2 will often be in total darkness, so cover bag 3 with an old towel so that all samples have similar light conditions.

5. Record your observations every day for two weeks to complete the chart.

N: no mould   **S:** some mould
L: lots of mould

Result

Did temperature affect the mould's growth?

_____

At which temperature did the mould grow best: warm, cool, or cold?

_____

Bag Day	1	2	3
1			
2			
3			
4			
5			
6			
7			
8			
9			
10			
11			
12			
13			
14			

Conclusion

The hypothesis was: _____

_____

My experiment _____ the hypothesis.
                    supported/did not support

4 Biodiversity: Connections

The interrelationships of living things within an ecosystem are very important. Animals and plants depend on one another in many ways. In this unit, you will look at a food web that occurs in a forest ecosystem, and examine the relationships between different organisms found in it.

After completing this unit, you will

- understand that living things depend on one another for many reasons, including for food.

- know some examples of special relationships.

We're the best partners in the world!

Vocabulary

carnivore: an animal that eats only meat

herbivore: an animal that eats only plants

omnivore: an animal that eats both plants and animals

human: omnivore

meat

vegetables

ISBN: 978-1-897457-78-8

Amazingly, plants make their own food with the help of the sun. However, some plants do not just produce; they also consume. They are "carnivores"! These "carnivores" even catch their prey in ways that are similar to how we catch ours.

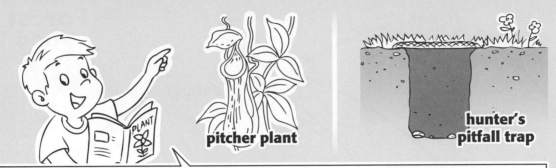

pitcher plant

hunter's pitfall trap

A pitcher plant traps its prey by attracting it to a "pitcher" that it cannot escape. The hunter's pitfall trap works in a similar way to trap animals.

A. **Identify each organism as a producer, consumer, or decomposer. Then write what type of consumer the consumers are.**

Types of Consumers:

carnivore
herbivore
omnivore

A _____ ; _____

B _____ ; _____

C _____ ; _____

D _____ ; _____

E _____ ; _____

F _____ ; _____

B. **Look at the forest food web. Answer the questions.**

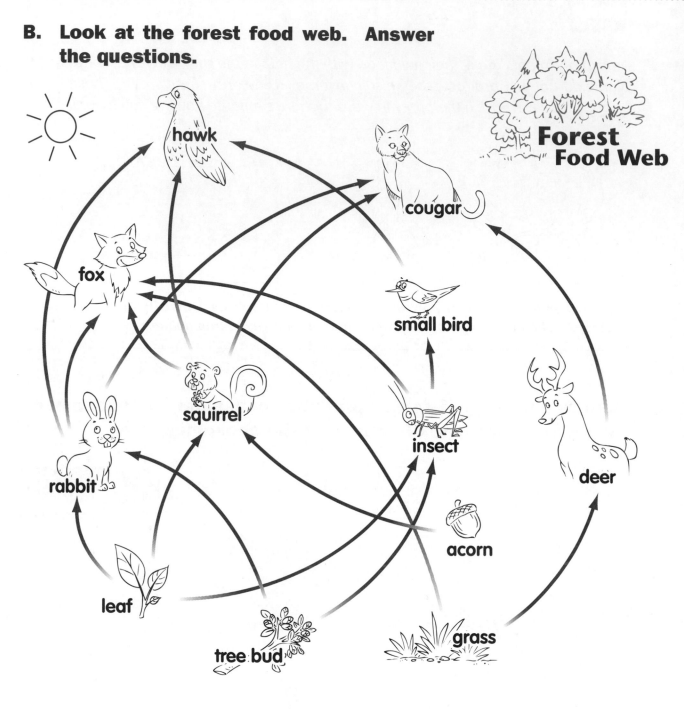

Forest Food Web

1. Fox eats: _____

2. Squirrel eats: _____

3. Using the food web, write a food chain that includes

   a. cougar: _____

   b. rabbit: _____

   c. leaf: _____

ISBN: 978-1-897457-78-8

C. Check or circle the correct answers to show the interrelationships within or between species.

1. **Interrelationships within Species**

Wolves travel in packs to

(A) defend their territory.

(B) get rid of that lonely feeling.

(C) raise their cubs.

(D) hunt large prey.

(E) huddle together for warmth.

2. **Interrelationships between Species**

a.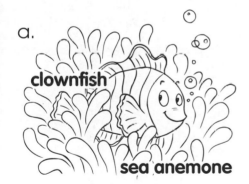

The clownfish protects its **eggs / fins** by laying them among the tentacles of the sea anemone, and in return the fish's bright colours attract **predators / prey** for the anemone to eat.

b.

Birds and bees get sustenance (food) from **plants / air** , but they also help carry **food / pollen** between plants.

ISBN: 978-1-897457-78-8

D. **Read the passage. Then identify the three types of symbiotic relationships and write the descriptions.**

Symbiosis:
Helping or Hurting?

Symbiosis is the dependence of one organism on another. There are three types of symbiotic relationships.

Commensalism: one organism benefits and the other neither benefits nor is harmed. The burdock plant relies on furry animals to disperse its thorny seeds. If an animal brushes a burdock, the animal's fur picks up the burdock seed and the animal unknowingly carries it to a new place.

Mutualism: both organisms benefit. When a bear eats blackberries, the bear fattens up for the long, cold winter, and the blackberry seeds are dispersed via the bear. When a sea anemone attaches itself to a hermit crab shell, it gets a free ride, and the hermit crab gets protection in the form of camouflage.

Parasitism: one organism benefits and the other is harmed. Some species of cuckoo bird lay their eggs in the nest of a different species, which will then raise the chicks at the expense of its own young.

ISBN: 978-1-897457-78-8

Three Types of Symbiotic Relationships

☺ benefits   ☻ neither benefits nor is harmed   ☹ is harmed

1.

• one ☺ and one ☻

furry animal

burdock plant

Description: _____

_____

_____

_____

2.

• both ☺

bear

blackberry bush

Description: _____

_____

_____

_____

3.

• one ☺ and one ☹

cuckoo

another bird's egg

cuckoo's egg

Description: _____

_____

_____

_____

_____

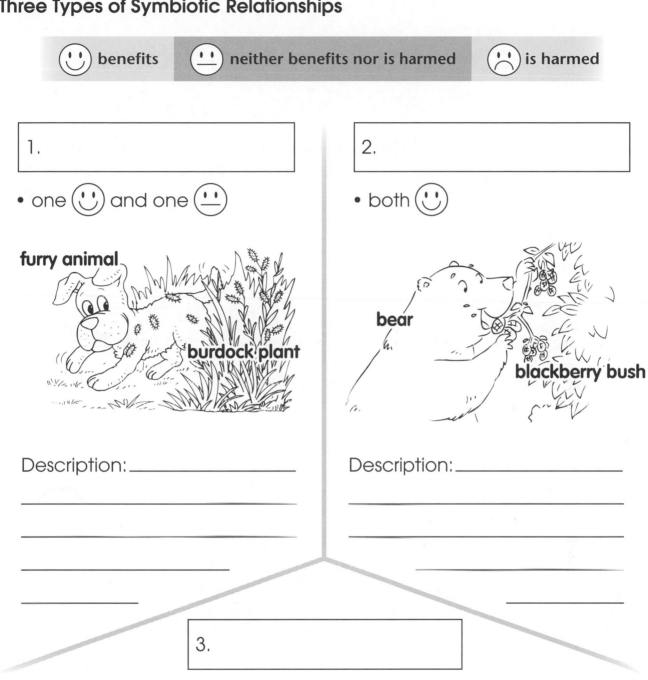

ISBN: 978-1-897457-78-8

5 Human Activities and Biodiversity

Human beings are a part of the biodiversity on Earth. We add to biodiversity, as any animal does, but we impact the level of biodiversity in negative ways, too. In this unit, you will examine different ways that humans influence and affect biodiversity.

After completing this unit, you will

- know that many kinds of scientists study biodiversity.
- understand that we benefit from biodiversity.
- understand that our activities affect biodiversity.

Do you know that we benefit from biodiversity?

panda (endangered animal)

Vocabulary

exploit: use fully for one's own benefit

endangered: at risk

conservation: the act of saving

ISBN: 978-1-897457-78-8

There are many examples of humans exploiting wildlife for their own gain. One of these examples is the illegal trade of wild animal parts. Below are some examples of the animals in danger due to people hunting them for their highly valued body parts.

elephant for ivory   **tiger for traditional medicines**   **rhinoceros for ivory**

Find out more about endangered animals on the Internet or in the library. Then think about things you can do to help save them.

A. Many different branches of science study biodiversity. Match the area of science with its work.

evolution   zoology
botany   genetics
conservation

1. _____ : the study of plants

2. _____ : the study of animals

3. _____ : the study of different species' evolutionary development

4. _____ : work to protect the natural world and the biodiversity within it

5. _____ : the study of genetic differences in members of the same animal or plant species

B. **How do we benefit from biodiversity? Read the clues to write the categories. Then sort each everyday product into the correct category and give your own example.**

Category	Everyday Product
clothing medicine food recreation household	tofu silk scarf traditional painkiller leather sofa skateboard

1. _____

- cotton T-shirt

- _____

- _____

2. _____

- campfire

- _____

- _____

3. _____

- ointment

- _____

- _____

4. _____

- butter

- _____

- _____

5. _____

- oak flooring

- _____

- _____

ISBN: 978-1-897457-78-8

C. **What do the people think about the development of a small, forested lot in the city? Write the letters to show what they say. Then add two more people who might have opinions about the issue and write what they might say.**

A "Preserve it as it is for its natural beauty."

B "It's the right size for a recreation complex."

Different matches are possible, so think carefully about your choices.

C "Preserve it as it is so that we don't disrupt any wildlife habitat."

D "A hotel would bring more tourists. Then the whole city will benefit."

E "Pave it so weeds won't be blown onto our property across the street."

F "Let's develop parts of the lot with homes but leave as many trees as possible in place."

Comments on the Development of a Forested Lot

People on the City Council Committee

☺ farmer: _____   ☺ landscape artist: _____

☺ scientist: _____   ☺ conservationist: _____

☺ developer: _____   ☺ restaurant owner: _____

☺ _____ : _____

_____

☺ _____ : _____

_____

D. Read the passage. Then fill in the blanks.

Biodiversity
Shapes Ways of Life

How people live is shaped by the biodiversity of where they live. Before contact with Europeans, Aboriginal peoples in what is now Canada depended mostly on the organisms around them.

On Canada's Pacific coast, the Haida's way of life revolved around water and cedar and spruce forests. The Haida built houses with cedar and spruce, made clothing from their bark and roots, and carved canoes and totem poles from the logs. They used their canoes to fish for salmon, their primary source of food.

In the Arctic, the Inuit primarily hunted and fished. Caribou and seal were used for food, clothing, blankets, tents, and boats. Oil from animal fat was used for cooking and lamps, whereas bones and ivory were used to make tools. Waterproof clothing was made from seal and walrus intestine. Houses were made from caribou hide in the summer and sod (grass and soil) in the winter.

ISBN: 978-1-897457-78-8

1. Aboriginal group: _____

   Living environment: _____

   _____

   Natural resources: _____

   _____

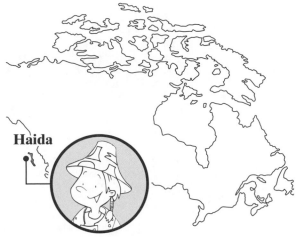

Haida

Used the natural resources for:

   • _____

   • _____

   • _____

   • _____

Circle the Haida's things:

spruce root hat

toboggan

kamiks

cedar bark canoe

cedar cape

2.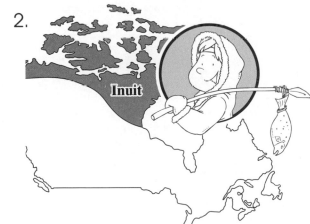

Inuit

   Aboriginal group: _____

   Living environment: _____

   _____

   Natural resources: _____

   _____

Give one example of what each animal part was used for:

   a. skin: _____   b. bone: _____

   c. fat: _____   d. intestine: _____

6 Biodiversity: Threats and Solutions

When a species is low in number, its diversity is threatened. When species drastically decline in numbers, or are even eliminated from an ecosystem, the health of that ecosystem is in peril. In this unit, you will see the different ways biodiversity is threatened, and what we can do about it.

After completing this unit, you will

- understand that our activities threaten biodiversity, but can also solve threats to and promote biodiversity.

- know how Canada categorizes threatened wildlife.

Don't worry. You'll be taken off the endangered list one day.

endangered animals

invasive species

grasshopper: destroys crops on a farm

Vocabulary

over fertilizing: happens when fertilizer is added to soil for short-term benefit, but does harm in the long term

invasive species: a non-native species that grows successfully and aggressively to dominate an area

ISBN: 978-1-897457-78-8

Extension

Wolves were once common in Yellowstone National Park in the United States, but people hunted them so much that they disappeared from the area.

Scientists studied the behaviour of wolves in other areas and worked to reintroduce them to the park. Their hard work paid off, as there are now once again wolves living in Yellowstone, and they have even been removed from the endangered species list.

A. **Draw lines to show how threats to biodiversity can be solved or prevented. Some threats may have more than one solution or prevention.**

Threats to Biodiversity

- pollution
- over hunting
- over fertilizing
- habitat destruction
- overuse of natural resources
- introduction of invasive species

Solutions to these Threats

- reintroduce native species
- improve wildlife habitats
- educate people
- reduce, reuse, recycle
- organic farming practices
- better rules and regulations

ISBN: 978-1-897457-78-8

B. Canada categorizes its threatened wildlife according to how much danger they are in. Complete the table by filling in the categories and the species on the list.

Category	Species
endangered extirpated threatened extinct special concern	Grey Fox Whooping Crane Oregon Lupine Blue Ash Labrador Duck

Wildlife Species at Risk

1. [ ] : may become threatened

Eastern Wolf, Lewis's Woodpecker, B_____ A_____

2. [ ] : likely to become endangered without intervention

Wood Bison, Soapweed, Goldenseal, G_____ F_____

3. [ ] : about to be extirpated or extinct

Vancouver Island Marmot, Yucca Moth, W_____ C_____

4. [ ] : no longer exists in the Canadian wild but occurs elsewhere

Grizzly Bear (in the prairies), Grey Whale, O_____ L_____

5. [ ] : no longer exists

Passenger Pigeon, L_____ D_____

ISBN: 978-1-897457-78-8

C. **Human interaction with wildlife is managed in many ways. Read the situations and decide how they promote biodiversity. Sort them into the correct boxes.**

A A law states that boats must turn off their motors when they are in the same area as whales.

B A class paints fish by sewer drains to remind people not to dump hazardous liquids.

C A scientist proposes a study to determine whether grey rat snakes are thriving in an area.

D A government department hires extra rangers when the provincial campsite is busier than usual.

E Every year, a conservation group counts the number of trumpeter swans that return to a river estuary.

F A teacher forms a nature club for interested students.

Promote Biodiversity by
Law:

_____

Promote Biodiversity by
Education/Example:

_____

ISBN: 978-1-897457-78-8

D. Read the passage. Then complete the information sheet and answer the question.

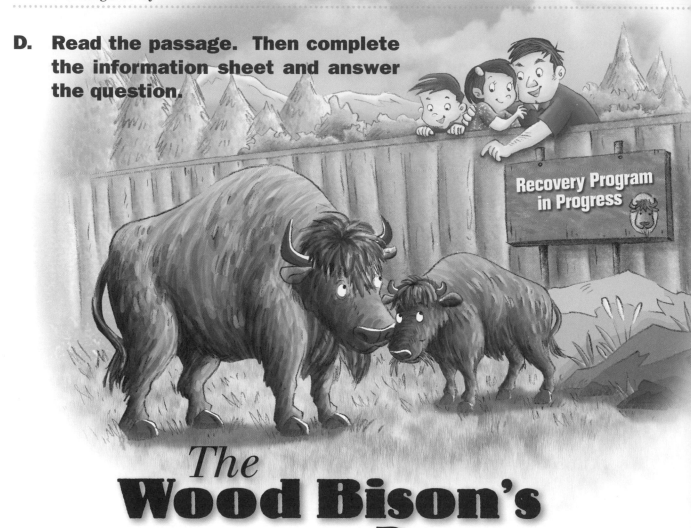

The
Wood Bison's
Recovery

The wood bison is the largest land animal in North America, weighing up to 1000 kilograms. Its habitat is mainly the meadows of the boreal forest in Canada's northwest where it travels in grazing herds, eating mostly grasses and sedges, but also eating tree leaves and bark. While close to 200 000 wood bison once roamed Canada's north, by the 1950s only 200 were left due largely to over hunting. During this time, the Canadian government considered the wood bison endangered and introduced recovery programs aimed at protecting it and reintroducing it into its former range. These programs have been successful; today there are over 4000 wood bison in the wild, and their range includes much of their traditional range: the Northwest Territories, the Yukon, British Columbia, Alberta, and Manitoba. Due largely to the efforts of the recovery programs, they have been moved from the endangered list to the threatened list.

ISBN: 978-1-897457-78-8

1. **Wood Bison**

size: _____

weight: _____

habitat: _____

_____

diet: _____

2.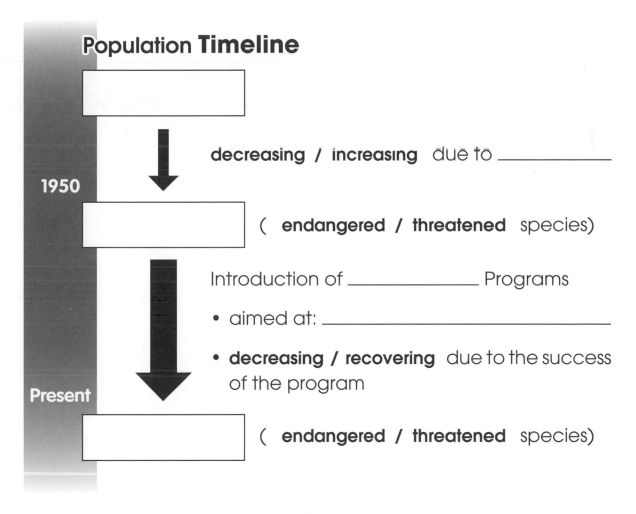

Population Timeline

[ ]

↓ **decreasing / increasing** due to _____

[ ] (**endangered / threatened** species)

1950

Introduction of _____ Programs

• aimed at: _____

• **decreasing / recovering** due to the success of the program

Present

[ ] (**endangered / threatened** species)

3. Suggest two ways to advance the wood bison recovery program's efforts.

_____

_____

_____

ISBN: 978-1-897457-78-8

Introduction

> How does biodiversity thrive in the different ecosystems around us? Does a small difference in location make a big difference in the level of biodiversity?

> Let's survey the living things in a particular ecosystem. Then we'll survey another ecosystem nearby and compare the findings.

> **Variables**
> • time
> • size

> We have to consider the variables and try to eliminate them from our experiment. To do that, let's observe both locations at the same time of day and make sure the locations are as close to the same size as possible.

Hypothesis

Different sites located close to each other can have different levels of biodiversity.

Materials
- *paper*
- *a pencil*

Steps

1. Decide on two locations for your experiment. They could be two different trees in a park or a patch of grass and a patch of flower garden. They should be as close to the same size as possible.

2. Decide on the length of time you will observe each location. Remember to observe the locations back to back so that both are observed at close to the same time of day.

3. Observe and record your results. Write how many different kinds of animals and plants you observed.

Location 1:
No. of different animals:
No. of different plants:

Location 2:
No. of different animals:
No. of different plants:

Result

Do different sites located close to each other have different levels of biodiversity?

_____

_____

Conclusion

The hypothesis was: _____

_____

My experiment _____ the hypothesis.
                    supported/did not support

Try to complete this review in **30 minutes**.

30minutes

This review consists of five sections, from A to E. The marks for each question are shown in parentheses. The circle at the bottom right corner is for the marks you get in each section. An overall record is on the last page of the review.

A.   Write T for true and F for false.

1.   Scientists have identified every species on Earth. **(2)**   _____

2.   A zoologist studies animals. **(2)**   _____

3.
An extirpated species is one that no longer exists on Earth. **(2)**

_____

4.
A butterfly is an invertebrate. **(2)**

_____

8

ISBN: 978-1-897457-78-8

B. Do the matching.

1.  (2)

2.  (2)

3.  (2)

4.  (2)

5.  (2)

- people hunt this animal for its tusks

- a biome with little biodiversity

- protected by an exoskeleton

- a biome with high biodiversity

- an omnivore

10

ISBN: 978-1-897457-78-8

C. Complete the chart on the classification of living things.

Kingdom

monerans   protists   fungi | 1. **(2)** | | 2. **(2)** |

| 3. **(2)** |

| 4. **(2)** |

Five Classes

- amphibians

    characteristic: a._____ **(2)**

    e.g. b._____ **(2)**

- fish

    characteristic: c._____ **(2)**

    e.g. d._____ **(2)**

- e._____ **(2)**

    characteristic: nurse young

    e.g. f._____ **(2)**

- g._____ **(2)**

    characteristic: have feathers

    e.g. h._____ **(2)**

- i._____ **(2)**

- characteristic: j._____ **(2)**

    e.g. snake

Insects (**2 each**)

(Check the insects.)

(A) butterfly

(B) mole

(C) beetle

(D) whale

(E) bee

(F) spider

Write three characteristics:

- _____ **(2)**

- _____ **(2)**

- _____ **(2)**

40

ISBN: 978-1-897457-78-8

D. Complete the food web. Then answer the questions.

1.

Food Web

seal
plankton
Arctic hare
polar bear

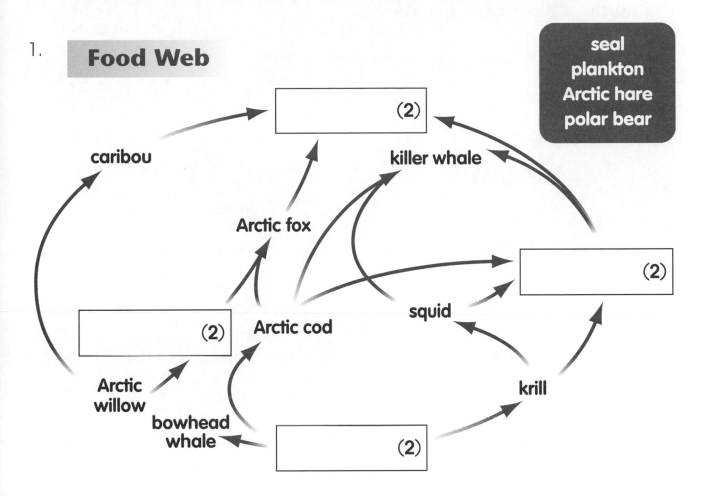

2. From above, name an example of

- a carnivore: _____ **(2)**

- a herbivore: _____ **(2)**

- a producer: _____ **(2)**

3. Name two abiotic elements in this biome.

_____ **(2)**

_____ **(2)**

4. In which biome does this food web exist? **(2)**

_____

5. Name one human threat to the biodiversity of the food web. **(2)**

_____

_____

E. Read about the yucca plant and the yucca moth. Answer the questions.

1. What is this relationship an example of? **(2)**

   (A) extirpation

   (B) mutualism

   (C) commensalism

Yucca Moth

Yucca Plant

2. Explain your choice. **(3)**

   _____

   _____

   _____

   - Yucca plants can only be pollinated by yucca moths.

   - Yucca moths lay their eggs in yucca plants' seed pods while pollinating; larvae eat only yucca seeds.

3. If the land where the yucca plant was on was to be developed for a housing project, what might

   a. happen to the plant and the moth? **(5)**

      _____

      _____

   b. ecologists think about the development? **(5)**

      _____

      _____

   c. construction workers think about the development? **(5)**

      _____

      _____

20

ISBN: 978-1-897457-78-8

My Record

Section **A**	8
Section **B**	10
Section **C**	40
Section **D**	22
Section **E**	20

Total

100

80-100

Great work! You really understand your science stuff! Research your favourite science topics at the library or on the Internet to find out more about the topics related to this section. Keep challenging yourself to learn more!

60-79

Good work! You understand some basic concepts, but try reading through the units again to see whether you can master the material! Go over the questions that you had trouble with to make sure you know the correct answers.

below 60

You can do much better! Try reading over the units again. Ask your parents or teachers any questions you might have. Once you feel confident that you know the material, try the review again. Science is exciting, so don't give up!

The Biologist

Jane Goodall is a famous biologist who knows a lot about chimpanzees. When she was a child, Goodall received a lifelike chimpanzee toy from her mother. That started her early love of animals. Today, she still has the toy with her in her home in London.

Goodall is best known for her study of the social and family lives of chimpanzees. She lived in the chimpanzee community in Gombe Stream National Park, Tanzania in 1960. Unlike other biologists, Goodall gave names to the chimpanzees she observed and studied instead of assigning each a number, and she was even accepted by the chimpanzees as one of them.

Goodall's major breakthrough in studying chimpanzees was the discovery of their ability to make tools. Although many animals had been observed using tools, only humans were thought to be able to make tools, and tool-making was considered the defining difference between humans and other animals.

Goodall is an animal welfare activist. Because of her love of animals, she campaigns against the use of animals in medical research, zoos, and sports.

ISBN: 978-1-897457-78-8

Cool Science Facts

1 Penguins are birds that can swim. Are there any fish that can fly?

flying fish

swimming bird

2 How does a Bullhorn Acacia hire the ant warriors to protect itself?

3 What is the "cousin" of a hippopotamus: a whale, a pig, or a cow?

4 What special parental care did gastric-brooding frogs give to their babies?

5 How long can a seed stay alive?

Find the answers on the next page.

ISBN: 978-1-897457-78-8

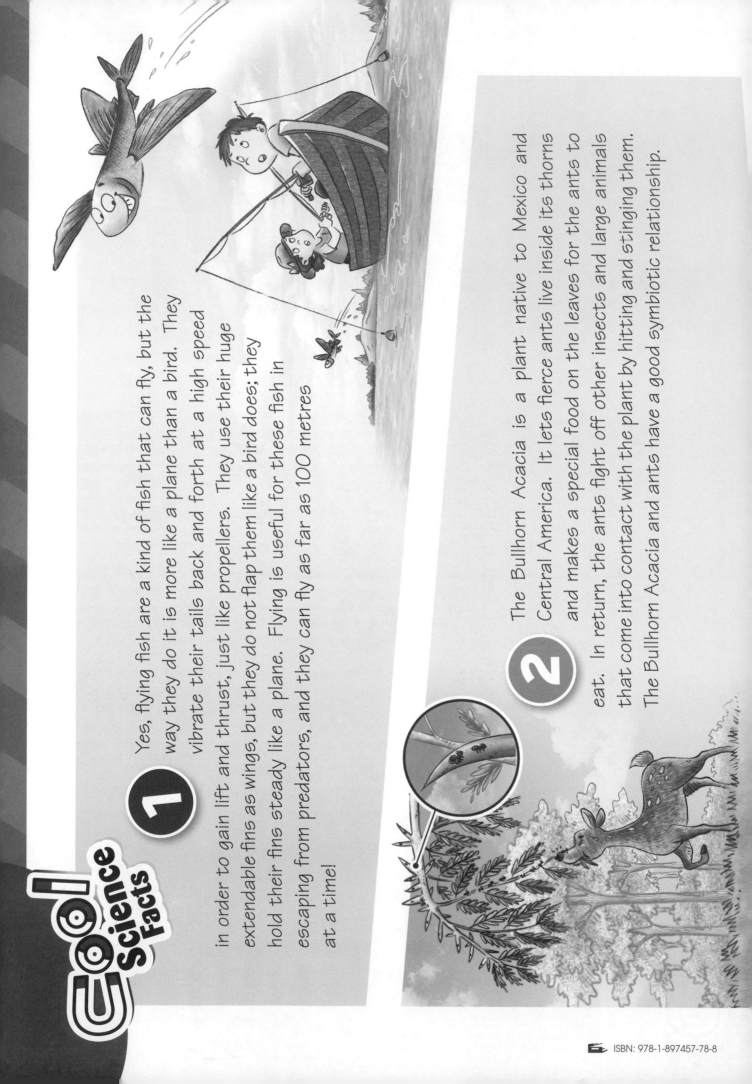

Cool Science Facts

1 Yes, flying fish are a kind of fish that can fly, but the way they do it is more like a plane than a bird. They vibrate their tails back and forth at a high speed in order to gain lift and thrust, just like propellers. They use their huge extendable fins as wings, but they do not flap them like a bird does; they hold their fins steady like a plane. Flying is useful for these fish in escaping from predators, and they can fly as far as 100 metres at a time!

2 The Bullhorn Acacia is a plant native to Mexico and Central America. It lets fierce ants live inside its thorns and makes a special food on the leaves for the ants to eat. In return, the ants fight off other insects and large animals that come into contact with the plant by hitting and stinging them. The Bullhorn Acacia and ants have a good symbiotic relationship.

ISBN: 978-1-897457-78-8

3

For many years, scientists had thought that hippos were related to pigs, but now scientists believe that hippos share a common ancestor with whales. Their ancestor was a 4-legged mammal that loved the water. It evolved into two different groups of animals: one that lost its legs and started living entirely in the water became whales, and another that stayed on land of which hippos are the only surviving descendants.

hippo — whale

Family Tree

4

A female gastric-brooding frog swallowed her clutch of eggs and the tadpoles hatched in her stomach. Scientists are interested in this form of reproduction, but unfortunately, this species is believed to be extinct.

gastric-brooding frog

Hi!

5

There are no definite answers, but it is believed that a seed can stay alive for several hundred years if it is kept in a dry and cold environment. Scientists planted a 2000-year-old palm seed, which was found near the Dead Sea in Israel. The seed grew into a healthy plant!

ISBN: 978-1-897457-78-8

ISBN: 978-1-897457-78-8

Section 2

Understanding Structures and Mechanisms

ISBN: 978-1-897457-78-8

1 Properties of Air

Understanding the properties of air allows us to understand its abilities and possibilities. In this unit, you will learn about the properties of air and see some everyday applications of these properties.

After completing this unit, you will

- understand that air has particular properties.
- know how we apply the properties of air in our lives.

Mom, can you see the power of air? Air can move this little windmill.

Vocabulary

gas: one of the three states of matter

oxygen: gas necessary for life

insulating: protecting against loss of heat

compressed: pushed to fit the same mass in a smaller space

mass: a measurement of matter

a warm blanket
(Air insulates.)

ISBN: 978-1-897457-78-8

Composition of Air

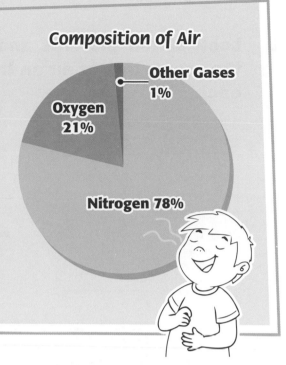

Air is not just one thing; it has many "ingredients". Nitrogen, a gas, is air's main ingredient. Oxygen is another important ingredient, though there is much less of it than nitrogen. Many other gases, including carbon dioxide, make up about 1% of air. One ingredient varies in its amount: the water vapour content of air depends on many factors occurring in the atmosphere. Without water vapour, we would not have clouds or rain.

A. Each picture shows a property of air. Write the property of air on the line. Then write one more example that shows that property.

Properties of Air

- takes up space
- pushes on objects
- has an insulating property

Air 1._____ .

e.g.

, _____

Air 2._____ .

e.g.

, _____

Air 3._____ .

e.g.

B. Look at the pictures and write the correct words. Then write the properties of air on the lines and give one more example for each.

1.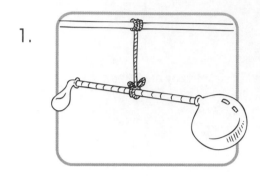

The fully inflated balloon weighs
_____ than the uninflated one.
<small>less/more</small>

➡️ Air has _____ .
<small>height/weight</small>

2.

Dandelion seeds fall _____ to the
<small>slowly/straight</small>
ground.

➡️ Air _____ things moving
<small>pushes/resists</small>
through it.

3.

A down sleeping bag traps _____
<small>warmth/cold</small>
inside and keeps cool air out.

➡️ Air has an _____ property.
<small>empty/insulating</small>

4.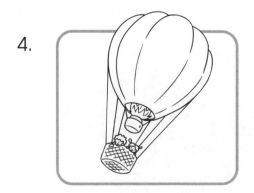

The hot air inside a hot-air balloon is
_____ dense than the colder air of
<small>less/more</small>
the atmosphere. Warm air _____
<small>rises/falls</small>
because it is lighter than cool air.

➡️ Air expands when _____ .
<small>heated/cooled</small>

ISBN: 978-1-897457-78-8

5.  Breathing in causes your lungs to fill up with

_____ .
water/air

➡ Air takes up _____ .
space/a challenge

6. 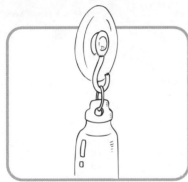 A scuba diver has enough air in a relatively small canister because air in the canister is

_____ .
compressed/heated

➡ Air can be _____ .
released/compressed

7. A suction cup stays firmly attached to a surface because the air pressure _____ the cup presses down on the
outside/inside
suction cup.

➡ Air _____ on objects.
pulls/pushes

Properties of Air ══════════ Examples

- _____ ; _____
- _____ ; _____
- _____ ; _____
- _____ ; _____
- _____ ; _____
- _____ ; _____
- _____ ; _____

C. Read the passage. Then answer the questions.

You know that warm air rises because it is lighter than cool air. However, when can you see this property at work?

If you were installing a wall-mounted air conditioner, where would you put it? It needs to be placed into a hole in the wall – yes, but where should the hole be made? It should be made at a height highest up from the floor. Why? The cool air from the air conditioner sinks, while warm air rises. If your air conditioner were close to the floor, only your legs would feel the cool air!

Hot Air Rises

Yummy!

Floor display freezers in grocery stores often do not have lids, yet the products inside remain frozen. Why? The cool air of the freezer stays in the freezer because it is much heavier than the warm air around it.

If you need a portable heater to keep you warm on cold winter nights, it is best to place it on the floor. Why? Warm air rises and will not sink below where the heater is placed.

ISBN: 978-1-897457-78-8

1. Draw a wall-mounted air conditioner in the correct box to show where it should be put in the room. Explain your choice.

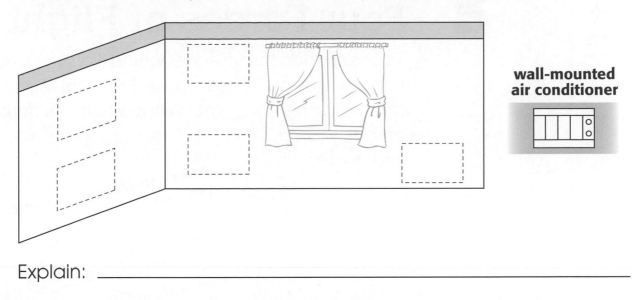

wall-mounted air conditioner

Explain: _____

_____

2. Draw to show where you would put a portable heater in the room below. Then explain your idea.

Explain: _____

_____

3. How can food be kept frozen in floor display freezers without lids?

_____

_____

2 Four Forces of Flight

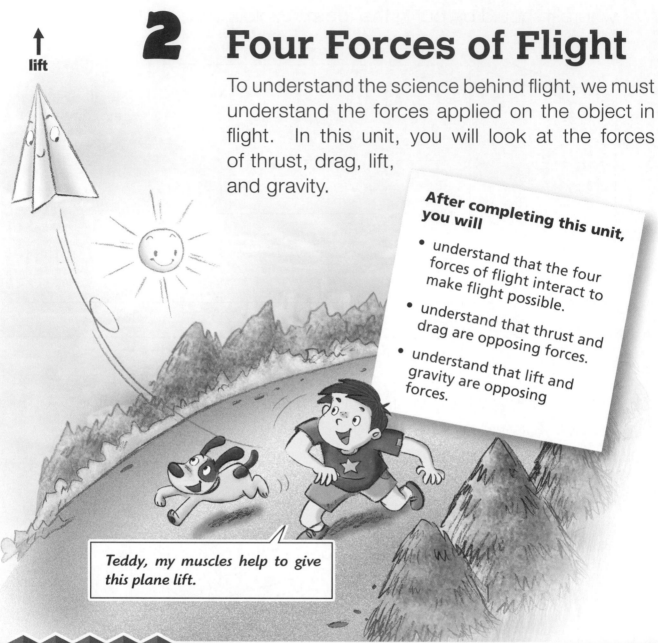

To understand the science behind flight, we must understand the forces applied on the object in flight. In this unit, you will look at the forces of thrust, drag, lift, and gravity.

After completing this unit, you will

- understand that the four forces of flight interact to make flight possible.
- understand that thrust and drag are opposing forces.
- understand that lift and gravity are opposing forces.

Teddy, my muscles help to give this plane lift.

Vocabulary

thrust: the force that causes forward movement

drag: the force that resists movement

lift: the force that causes an object to rise

gravity: the force that pulls objects to the Earth

altitude: one's vertical position in the air in relation to the ground or sea

ISBN: 978-1-897457-78-8

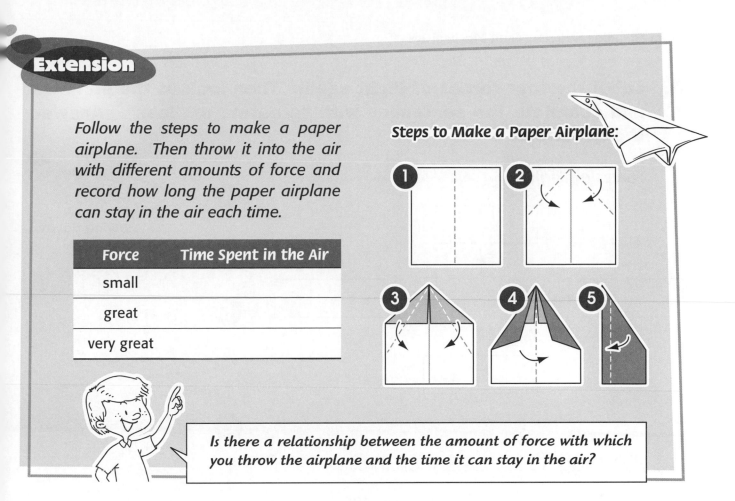

Follow the steps to make a paper airplane. Then throw it into the air with different amounts of force and record how long the paper airplane can stay in the air each time.

Steps to Make a Paper Airplane:

Force	Time Spent in the Air
small	
great	
very great	

Is there a relationship between the amount of force with which you throw the airplane and the time it can stay in the air?

A. **The arrows show the direction of the two pairs of opposing forces. Colour one pair of arrows one colour and the other pair a different colour. Then label the arrows.**

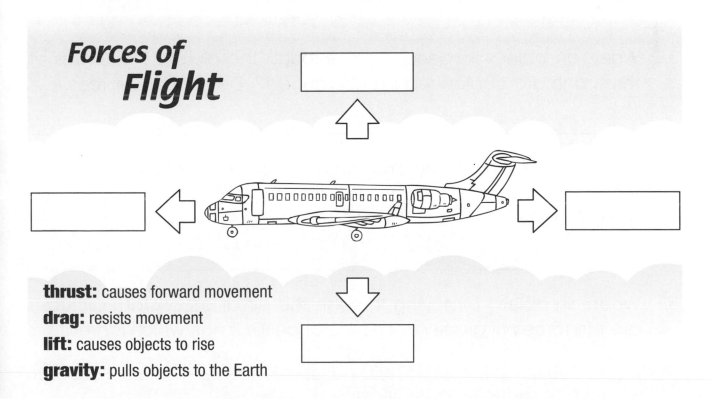

Forces of
Flight

thrust: causes forward movement

drag: resists movement

lift: causes objects to rise

gravity: pulls objects to the Earth

B. **Label the four forces of flight again. Then look at the pictures and complete the sentences with "greater" or "less". Answer the questions.**

1. *Forces of Flight*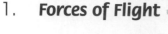

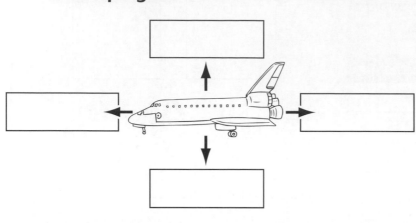

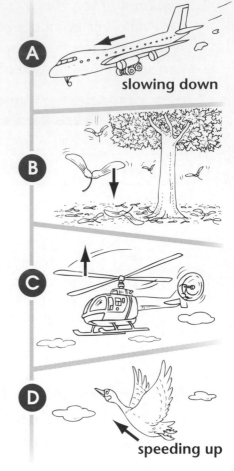

A slowing down

B

C

D

speeding up

2. (A) Drag is _____ than thrust.

(B) Gravity is _____ than lift.

(C) Gravity is _____ than lift.

(D) Drag is _____ than thrust.

3. When an object is speeding up through the air, are the forces of thrust and drag balanced or unbalanced? Describe the forces.

_____

4. If the forces of thrust and drag on an object are balanced, but the forces of gravity and lift are unbalanced, what two things could be happening?

_____

5. When an object is moving through the air at a constant altitude, are the forces of gravity and lift balanced? If not, which is greater?

_____

  ISBN: 978-1-897457-78-8

C. **Complete what the pilot says. Then write the source of thrust for each flying machine.**

Thrust comes from whatever _____ flying objects or animals.

propels/resists

1. _____

2. _____

3. _____

4. _____

D. **Check the correct answer. Then fill in the boxes with "drag" or "gravity".**

Drag comes from _____ .

(A) air resistance

(B) gravity

(C) treetops

1. [_____]

Air slows down the parachutist from the drop.

2. [_____]

E. Read the passage. Then answer the questions.

Sam, this bicycle with low handlebars allows you to move faster than one with handlebars that require you to sit upright.

Air Resistance
Is a Drag

Most vehicles are designed to reduce air resistance in order to move faster. When a vehicle reduces its air resistance, it can achieve a certain speed using less force than it otherwise would. Imagine you are a cyclist getting ready for a race. You have two bicycles to choose from: one has handlebars that allow you to bend so that your chest almost touches your knees; the other has handlebars that require you to sit upright. Which bicycle would you choose?

On the other hand, parachutists need air resistance to land safely. Parachutes, in fact, are designed to create the perfect amount of air resistance for what is being dropped, be it a person, a space capsule, or a box of food. Some planes deploy horizontal parachutes, or drag chutes, to brake after they have landed. Some race cars do the same after they have crossed the finish line. These vehicles use air resistance to stop moving.

     ISBN: 978-1-897457-78-8

1. Draw the correct arrow to show the amount and direction of drag on each vehicle and each parachute. Then answer the questions.

Drag

greatest

great

least

a. The vehicles are moving forward at the same speed.

b. Which vehicle has the least drag? Why do you think so?

_____

_____

c. The parachutists jump from the same plane at the same time.

d. Which parachutist reaches the ground safely first? Why?

_____

_____

2. Draw to show how this plane deploys a drag chute to brake when it is landing.

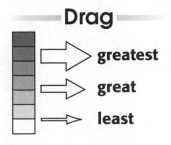

3 Flight: Moving Through Air

Birds and airplanes have special designs to help them fly, take off, land, or even turn in the air. In this unit, you will learn what the term "streamlined" means and see the ways an airplane can accomplish different movements in the air.

Teddy, let me show you how to yaw!

After completing this unit, you will

- understand that different movements in the air can be achieved by creating unbalanced forces.

- understand that the four forces of flight can be altered to achieve different movements in the air.

A yaw is the side-to-side movement of the plane's nose.

Vocabulary

pitch: climb or descend

roll: turn over

yaw: turn to the left or right

streamlined: shape of an object that reduces drag, as it provides the least air resistance

streamlined helmet

ISBN: 978-1-897457-78-8

Extension

Water and air are fluids. They both resist objects moving through them, which is a force called drag. Fish and birds have bodies specially designed to decrease drag so that they can move freely through fluids. We have learned from fish and birds to design many items that reduce resistance. Take a look at your cycling helmet. Can you see that its shape is curved and smooth? Try riding your bike with a cardboard box over your helmet and compare it with wearing just your helmet. You should feel a big difference in the amount of drag as you ride.

A. Circle the correct words. Then check the streamlined objects.

A **boxy / streamlined** shape is one that reduces drag the most by **increasing / reducing** air or water resistance.

Streamlined Objects

A

B

C

D

E

B. Label the parts that control the movement of a plane. Fill in the blanks and colour the parts to match the descriptions. Then name the parts that are at work and the motion they allow.

rudder – at the rear of the vertical stabilizer
ailerons – at the rear of the wings
elevators – at the rear of the horizontal stabilizers

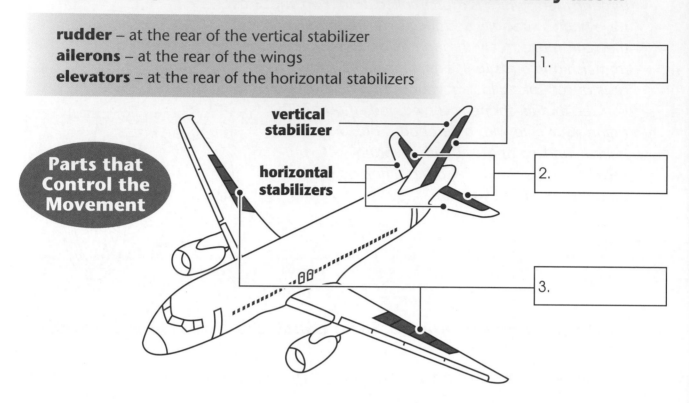

Parts that Control the Movement

vertical stabilizer

horizontal stabilizers

1.

2.

3.

4.　The Three Basic Motions of a Plane – Roll, Yaw, and Pitch

    a.　R_____ motion is an up and down movement of the wings, which is controlled by the _____ . The ailerons work in opposition. When the right aileron goes up, the left aileron goes _____ .

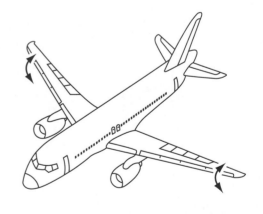

    b.　Y_____ motion is a side-to-side movement of the nose of the aircraft, which is controlled by the _____ . The rudder can be moved left or right.

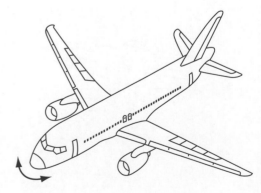

c. P_____ motion is an up and down movement of the nose of the aircraft, which is controlled by the _____ . The elevators work in pairs. When the right elevator goes up, the left elevator goes _____ .

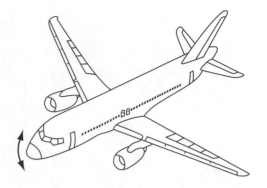

5.  _____ motion   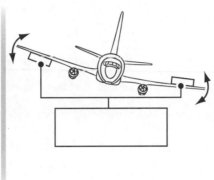 _____ motion   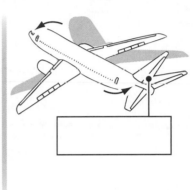 _____ motion

C. Use the given words to answer the questions about the forces of flight.

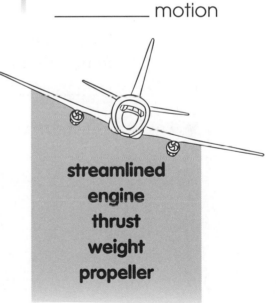

streamlined
engine
thrust
weight
propeller

1. What two things might provide thrust on a real airplane?

   _____

2. Which shape helps reduce the force of drag?

   _____

3. The difference between a paper airplane and a wooden airplane is the _____ of the material.

4. A paper airplane blown off the hand has less _____ than one that is thrown using the arm.

ISBN: 978-1-897457-78-8

D. Read the passage. Then answer the questions.

Get to Know the
Snowbirds

Have you ever been to an air show? If you have, then you have probably seen the Snowbirds fly in amazing formations. These nine planes fly at speeds between 180 kilometres and 590 kilometres an hour while performing acrobatic tricks involving extreme rolling, pitching, and yawing. Even while performing their most daring tricks, they often fly only 1.2 metres apart.

All Snowbird pilots are Royal Canadian Air Force pilots. The planes they pilot are called CT-114 Tutors. All are painted with the same colours in the same design: a red underside with a white top half and a blue stripe running across it. Each plane weighs 3260 kilograms and has a fuel tank that holds 1173 litres of fuel. Its wingspan (from one wing tip to the other) is 11.12 m, its height, 2.82 m, and its length, 9.75 m. While these planes may seem big and heavy, they are specially crafted to manoeuvre with amazing precision.

ISBN: 978-1-897457-78-8

1. Colour the plane and write the information.

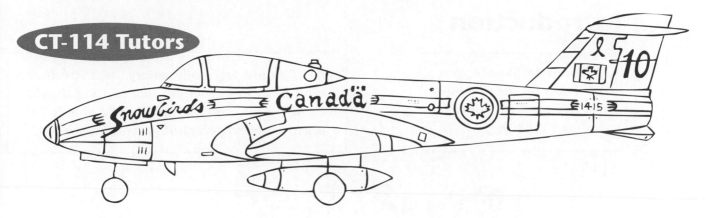

CT-114 Tutors

Pilot: from _____

Weight: _____

Fuel Tank Capacity: _____

Speed Range: _____
(during tricks)

Dimensions

Wingspan: _____

Height: _____

Length: _____

2. Write the movements of the planes.

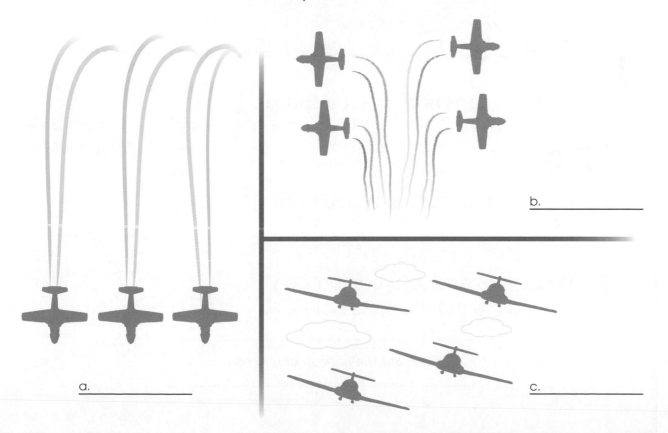

a. _____

b. _____

c. _____

ISBN: 978-1-897457-78-8

Experiment

Introduction

It's hard to believe that air takes up space when we can't see it or feel it unless it's moving.

Is an empty jug really empty, or is it full of air? If air does take up space, a jug should be full of air, and we shouldn't be able to fill it with anything else until we let the air out.

If it is empty, then we should be able to easily inflate a balloon inside the jug.

Hypothesis

Air   takes / does not take   up space.

Steps

1. Push the body of the balloon into the bottle.

2. Wrap the end of your balloon around the mouth of the bottle.

Stretch out the balloon before you use it.

Materials

- *a plastic jug or bottle*
- *an uninflated balloon*
- *a pin*

ISBN: 978-1-897457-78-8

3. Blow into the balloon to inflate it.

4. Record your observations.

5. Poke some holes in the bottle with a pin. (Ask your parents for assistance if needed.)

a hole

6. Blow into the balloon to inflate it.

7. Draw the balloon at each stage.

Result

1. Could you inflate the balloon when there were

    a. no holes in the jug?   _____

    b. holes in the jug?   _____

2. Explain.

    _____

Observations

Before (without holes)

After (with holes)

Conclusion

The hypothesis was: _____

_____

My experiment _____ the hypothesis.
                    supported/did not support

ISBN: 978-1-897457-78-8

4 Bernoulli's Principle

To understand flight, you must understand Bernoulli's principle. In this unit, you will examine this principle and see how it affects airplane and animal wings. You will also see how Bernoulli's principle acts on an airfoil to make flight possible.

After completing this unit, you will

- understand Bernoulli's principle.
- understand how lift happens.
- know the shape of an airfoil.

greater pressure (on the underside)

Sam, we can all see that you know how to make the paper rise. You can stop...

wings: an example of an airfoil

vocabulary

air pressure: amount of pressure exerted by air

airfoil: a curved shape that helps generate lift

exert: apply (force)

ISBN: 978-1-897457-78-8

Extension

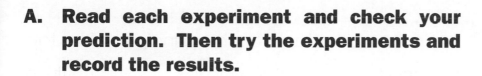

Leonardo da Vinci was a painter, sculptor, mathematician, engineer, and scientist born in Italy on April 15, 1452. Though he was born long before human flight was a reality, he was fascinated with flight, and studied birds extensively. He also drew many plans for flying machines that resemble today's helicopters and hang-gliders. While these plans were visionary, few were practical, and almost none would have been able to fly had he constructed them.

A. Read each experiment and check your prediction. Then try the experiments and record the results.

1. Blow under the paper.

   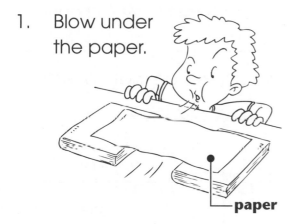

   paper

   Prediction:

   (A) The paper sinks down between the books.

   (B) The paper rises.

   Result: _____

2. Blow air between two balloons.

   Prediction:

   (A) The balloons move away from each other.

   (B) The balloons move closer to each other.

   Result: _____

B. Fill in the blanks to reveal Bernoulli's principle and complete the paragraph. Then complete the diagram with the words in bold.

wings	faster	speed	above	lower	lift	slower

Bernoulli's Principle

David Bernoulli, a scientist, proposed that changes in air 1._____ are related to changes in air pressure. 2._____ moving air exerts **lower** pressure than **slower** moving air.

An airplane's 3._____ take advantage of this principle. The top surface of a wing is curved and the end of the wing is 4._____ than its front edge. The air 5._____ the wing travels **faster** over a curved surface than the air below the wing. The 6._____ air has **higher** pressure than the faster air, and it is this pressure difference that generates 7._____ .

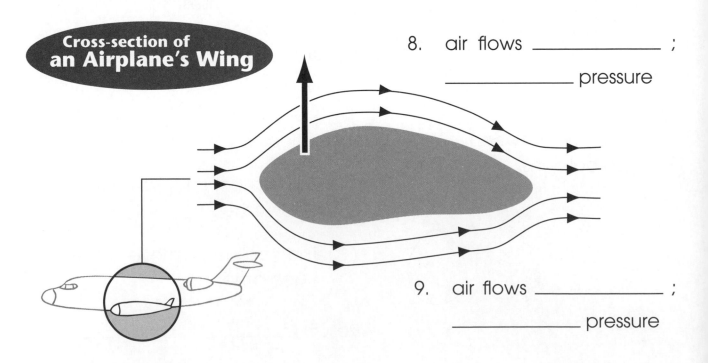

Cross-section of an Airplane's Wing

8. air flows _____ ;
_____ pressure

9. air flows _____ ;
_____ pressure

C. Fill in the blanks to find out about airfoils. Then check the pictures that are examples of airfoils.

natural	lift	Bernoulli's	air	airfoil

An Airfoil

An airplane's wing is not the only object that

takes advantage of 1._____ principle.

A wing's special shape is called an 2._____ , and many other

objects, both 3._____ and human-made, share this shape in order

to generate 4._____ or move through 5._____ .

Examples of Airfoils

6.

D. Read the passage. Name and colour the parts that each aircraft uses to generate thrust. Then draw arrows to show the direction of thrust and lift and complete the descriptions.

Propeller planes, jet planes, and helicopters all have different methods of generating thrust and lift.

A propeller plane has a propeller that spins, making air flow faster in front of it than behind it; faster moving air equals lower air pressure, and the plane moves forward.

A jet plane, on the other hand, has jet engines into which air flows. The air is mixed with fuel inside the engines and ignited. The resulting exploding gas travels out of the engine, thrusting the plane forward. For both propeller and jet planes, it is this forward motion that forces air to flow over the wings fast enough to generate lift.

A helicopter's rotors generate both lift and thrust. The main rotor rotates with such speed that air flows fast enough over the rotor's blades to generate lift, allowing the helicopter to take off vertically, unlike planes, which need a runway. The rotor is adjustable, and this is what provides thrust. The tail rotor keeps the helicopter's fuselage from rotating with the main rotor and also works in much the same way as the main rotor to generate lift and thrust.

          ISBN: 978-1-897457-78-8

1.

Propeller Plane

Once the propeller spins, the air in the front moves

_____ than the air at the back. This causes _____ to move
faster/slower   drag/thrust

the plane forward. Then the wings of the plane create _____ .
weight/lift

2.

main _____

tail _____

Helicopter

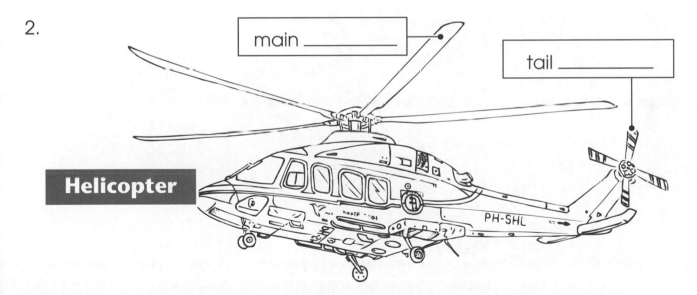

The main rotor's rotations generate _____ , while the helicopter pilot
lift/thrust

adjusts the rotor to generate _____ . The tail rotor also provides
thrust/weight

the helicopter with lift and thrust, as well as preventing the fuselage from

_____ with the main rotor.
leaving/rotating

5 Living Things and Flight

Most birds, insects, and even some mammals can fly. Some plants' seeds also float like balloons, or rotor down like helicopters. In this unit, you will examine flight adaptations and see how our flying machines mimic nature.

flying squirrel

Look! I can glide freely through the air!

After completing this unit, you will

- know some of the possible reasons for flight adaptations.

- learn about some flight mechanisms of living things.

- have compared human-made flying machines with nature's flyers.

Vocabulary

adaptation: a change to better suit an environment

predator: an animal that hunts for food

prey: an animal that is hunted for food

ascend: move upward (into the air)

predator

prey

  ISBN: 978-1-897457-78-8

Some animals have wings to fly, but over time have lost the ability. When we think of what makes a bird a bird, is it only the ability to fly? There is so much more to birds than flight! They have feathers, beaks, and they lay eggs. Have you ever seen any of the birds on the right? How do they move?

kiwi

ostrich

emu

penguin

A. Fill in the blanks to show how living things gained flight to adapt to their environments.

home	predators	food	migrate	prey	mate

Reasons for Flight Adaptations

to stabilize a flight and find a 1._____

to search for 2._____

to catch 3._____

to find a new 4._____

to 5._____

to escape from 6._____

B. Fill in the blanks and match the living things with their adaptations for flight. Write the letters.

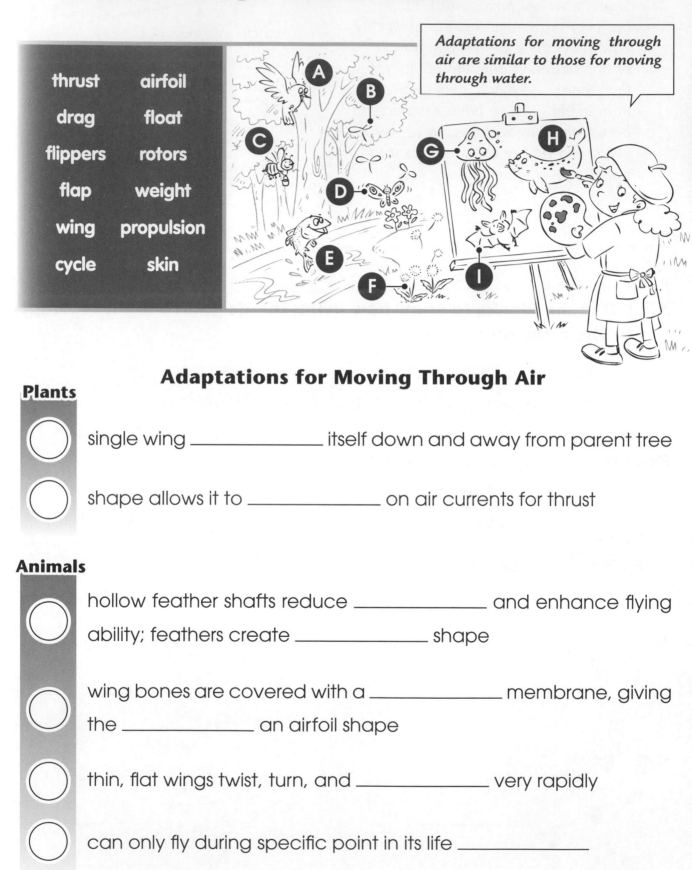

Adaptations for moving through air are similar to those for moving through water.

thrust   airfoil

drag   float

flippers   rotors

flap   weight

wing   propulsion

cycle   skin

Adaptations for Moving Through Air

Plants

○ single wing _____ itself down and away from parent tree

○ shape allows it to _____ on air currents for thrust

Animals

○ hollow feather shafts reduce _____ and enhance flying ability; feathers create _____ shape

○ wing bones are covered with a _____ membrane, giving the _____ an airfoil shape

○ thin, flat wings twist, turn, and _____ very rapidly

○ can only fly during specific point in its life _____

ISBN: 978-1-897457-78-8

Adaptations for Moving Through Water

Animals

the tail swishes from side to side to produce _____ and the fins pulled close to its body reduce _____

has adapted _____ , the same method of thrust that a jet airplane uses

the front _____ are like wings to propel it through the water

C. Draw lines to match the pictures with the correct descriptions. Then draw the tail of the bird in each stage of flight.

• diving

• taking off

A bird's tail acts like an airplane's elevators. It bends down when diving or landing, and bends up for taking off or climbing.

Taking off

Gliding

Landing

ISBN: 978-1-897457-78-8

D. Read the passage. Then answer the questions.

Nature's Most Versatile Flyers:

Hummingbirds

There are many species of hummingbirds. The smallest warm-blooded vertebrate on Earth, the Bee Hummingbird, is about 5.7 centimetres long, weighs less than a penny, and is found in Cuba and the Caribbean. The Ruby-throated Hummingbird is the most common hummingbird species in North America.

As its name suggests, the Ruby-throated Hummingbird has a swath of red-coloured feathers across its throat, though this is mostly found in the males. Both males and females have feathers of green, white, and black. On average, Ruby-throated Hummingbirds are 8.9 centimetres long, weigh 3.1 grams, and have a wingspan of 10 cm. In order to fly quickly (about 55 kilometres per hour) and to manoeuvre well, a hummingbird beats its wings in a figure-8 motion about 53 times per second. This distinctive wing motion is possible because a hummingbird's wings are attached to its torso only at its shoulder joints, unlike other birds. It is also this motion that allows a hummingbird to hover and fly backwards.

ISBN: 978-1-897457-78-8

1. Fill in the correct information.

Bee Hummingbird

- weight: _____
- length: _____
- size: _____
- found in: _____

Ruby-throated Hummingbird

- weight: _____
- length: _____
- wingspan: _____
- found in: _____

2. Read the descriptions. Then draw lines to match the descriptions with the correct movements of a hummingbird.

Flying forwards:

flapping its wings up and down • like other birds

Hovering:

moving its wings rapidly back • and forth in a figure-8 motion

Flying backwards:

the body is positioned vertically and the wings reach strongly • back, down and up, making an oval in the air

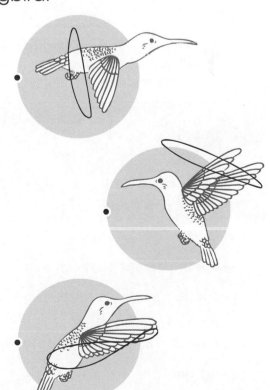

ISBN: 978-1-897457-78-8

6 Flight and Society

Human flight has changed our world. In this unit, you will see that human flight has developed over a short period of time and that many different devices have been developed. You will also examine the benefits and costs of flight to communities.

After completing this unit, you will

- know some important events in the history of human flight.

- know some purposes of human flight.

- understand that human flight can have both benefits and costs.

It's efficient to spray farmer's fields with fertilizers using me – a small propeller plane.

Vocabulary

seaplane

seaplane: plane that can take off from and land on water

propeller plane: smaller plane that has the source of thrust from an engine-powered propeller

jet plane: plane that has the source of thrust from jet engines; can be very large

aviation: area of science that has to do with aircraft

ISBN: 978-1-897457-78-8

Many northern Canadian communities can only be accessed by road vehicles in the winter months, when temporary roads are carved from ice and snow. In the spring, summer, and fall months, they are only accessible by plane. These communities are called fly-in communities. Without flight, they could not stock their grocery stores, send their children to schools in larger towns, have visitors, or transport people who need medical attention.

A. Complete the timeline to show the development of human flight.

hot-air balloon
Wright Brothers   1910
moon   Russia   kites
helicopter   glider

Events in Aviation

400 BCE — China:

first _____

1783 — Montgolfier Brothers (France):

first _____

1891 — Otto Lilienthal (Germany):

first long distance _____

1903 — _____ (U.S.A.): first airplane

— France: first seaplane

1936 — Germany: first practical _____

1961 — Yuri Gagarin (_____):
first person in space

1969 — Neil Armstrong (U.S.A.):
first person on the _____

B. **Check the correct letters. Then answer the question.**

Best Aviation Device for Each Purpose

1. mountain search and rescue:

 (A)  (B)  (C)

2. cross-Atlantic travel:

    (A) hot-air balloon   (B) helicopter   (C) jet airplane

3. transporting fish farm workers

    (A) glider   (B) seaplane   (C) spacecraft

4. spraying farmer's fields

    (A) propeller plane   (B) helicopter   (C) kite

5.

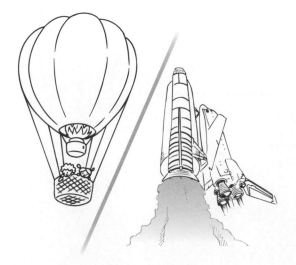

Name one purpose for each device:

a. a hot-air balloon

_____

b. a spacecraft

_____

ISBN: 978-1-897457-78-8

C. **Describe one benefit and one cost in each scenario that would affect at least one group of people listed below.**

people who might be affected

anglers   tourists   home builders   schoolteachers
travellers   business owners   residents

An international airport is being built to serve a growing city. The area it is in is easy to access for all residents, but it is very close to homes and schools.

Benefit: _____

_____

_____

Cost: _____

_____

_____

scenerio 2

A seaplane company that operates across the river from the fishery and community it serves is introducing more frequent flights. On that same river is a wilderness resort and a conservation area.

Benefit: _____

_____

_____

Cost: _____

_____

_____

D. Read the passage. Choose the appropriate aircraft for each situation. Then write one advantage and one disadvantage for using the aircraft.

Flying: the Benefits and the Risks

Human flight has made life easier, safer, and more efficient, but flight has its drawbacks, too.

Millions of people travel by plane for fun or for business. Flying is fast, and allows people to travel anywhere in the world. However, infectious diseases can be spread globally easier by infected airplane passengers going from place to place.

Aircraft provide fast transportation to the hospital for badly injured people. While these aircraft save lives, they often fly low in urban areas, creating noise pollution.

Aircraft used to dust crops with pesticides and fertilizers make the process fast and easy, but sprayed chemicals can get onto nearby wild plants, harming those plants and wasting chemicals.

Aircraft are used to locate forest fires, dump large amounts of water or chemicals onto those fires, and drop firefighters into remote areas to fight fires from the ground. Like all aircraft, though, they cause air and noise pollution. They also use an enormous amount of fuel, which harms the environment.

ISBN: 978-1-897457-78-8

Types of Aircraft

Bombardier 415
- can scoop about 6000 L of water in a short time

Airbus A380
- the largest passenger airliner with about 555 seats

Antonov An-2
- slow flying and often has spraying systems built into its wings

Sikorsky S-76
- can land vertically, so can land on hospital roofs

Use of Aircraft 😊 : advantage ☹ : disadvantage

1. For Fun/Business: _____

   😊 : _____
   ☹ : _____

2. For Emergency: _____

   😊 : _____
   ☹ : _____

3. In Agriculture: _____

   😊 : _____
   ☹ : _____

4. For Fighting Wildfires: _____

   😊 : _____
   ☹ : _____

ISBN: 978-1-897457-78-8

Introduction

Bernoulli's principle states that the faster air moves, the less pressure it exerts. This principle helps explain how airplanes and birds gain lift, but is there a way to see the principle at work in my own home?

Hypothesis

Slow-moving air exerts more pressure than fast-moving air.

Steps

Materials

- *a hair dryer*
- *a ping pong ball*

1. Hold the hair dryer with its opening pointing up towards the ceiling. Turn it on.

2. Place the ping pong ball in the stream of air.

For this experiment, be sure to set the hair dryer to "cold".

ISBN: 978-1-897457-78-8

3. Record your observations by drawing a picture that shows the hair dryer's stream of air and the ping pong ball.

Result

Did the ping pong ball float?

_____ (If you answered "yes", continue; if "no", skip to conclusion.)

Colour the fast-moving air red and the slow moving air blue. Then answer the question and circle the correct words.

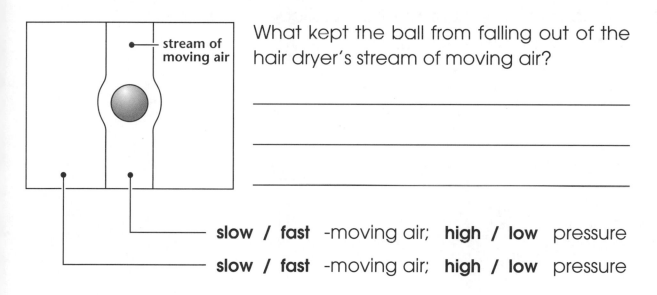

What kept the ball from falling out of the hair dryer's stream of moving air?

_____

_____

_____

slow / fast -moving air; **high / low** pressure

slow / fast -moving air; **high / low** pressure

Conclusion

The hypothesis was: _____

_____

My experiment _____ the hypothesis.

supported/did not support

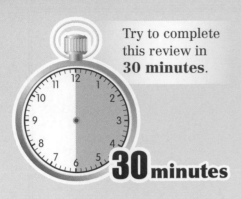

Try to complete this review in **30 minutes**.

30 minutes

This review consists of five sections, from A to E. The marks for each question are shown in parentheses. The circle at the bottom right corner is for the marks you get in each section. An overall record is on the last page of the review.

A. Write T for true and F for false.

1. Oxygen is a gas in the air that is essential to life. **(2)** _____

2. Altitude is the measure of one's vertical position in relation to the sky or sea. **(2)** _____

3.    All birds can fly. **(2)**

_____

4.    A streamlined shape reduces drag, as it provides the most air resistance. **(2)**

_____

8

ISBN: 978-1-897457-78-8

B. Do the matching.

1.

2.

3.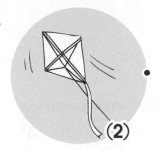

4.

5.

- circa 400 BCE; first flown in China

- Italian inventor and artist

- spinning propeller generates thrust

- an airfoil shape in nature

- air resistance allows it to fall slowly

10

ISBN: 978-1-897457-78-8

C. Write the properties of air with the help of the clues. Then answer the questions.

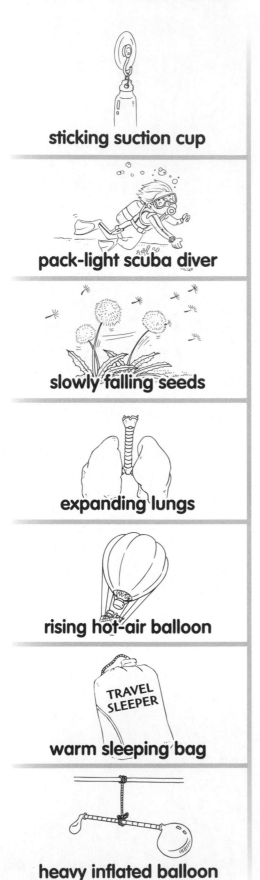

sticking suction cup

pack-light scuba diver

slowly falling seeds

expanding lungs

rising hot-air balloon

warm sleeping bag

TRAVEL SLEEPER

heavy inflated balloon

1. Properties of Air: (**3 marks each**)

- _____

- _____

- _____

- _____

- _____

- _____

- _____

2. There is no air in space. Do you think that...

   a. airplanes could generate lift in space? Why or why not? (**4**)

      _____

      _____

      _____

   b. an astronaut could fly a kite in space? Why or why not? (**4**)

      _____

      _____

      _____

29

ISBN: 978-1-897457-78-8

D. Label the parts that control the movement of a plane and the four forces of flight. Then answer the questions.

The Parts

ailerons   elevators   rudder

Forces

lift   thrust   drag   gravity

1.

Four Forces of Flight

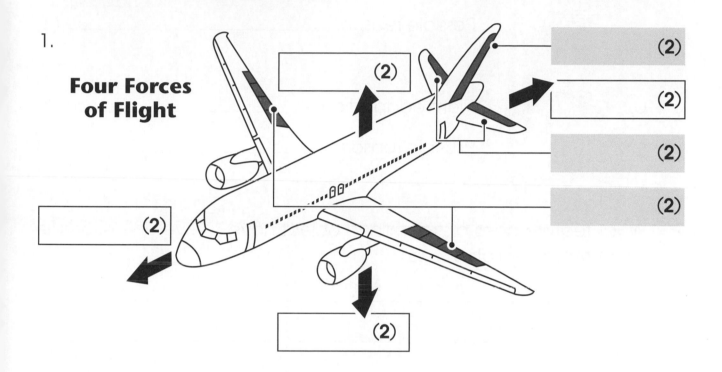

(2)

(2)

(2)

(2)

(2)

(2)

(2)

2.   What happens to the plane if:

   a.   thrust is greater than drag? **(3)**   _____

   b.   gravity is greater than lift? **(3)**   _____

   c.   drag is greater than thrust? **(3)**   _____

3.   What do we call the shape of an airplane's wing? Why? Name and state the principle this shape takes advantage of. **(4)**

   _____

   _____

   _____

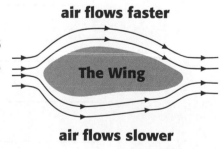

air flows faster

The Wing

air flows slower

27

ISBN: 978-1-897457-78-8

E. Answer the questions.

1. Describe the flight adaptation of each living thing and write one possible reason for it.

   a.   Flight adaptation: _____ (**3**)

        Possible reason: _____ (**3**)

   b.   Flight adaptation: _____ (**3**)

        Possible reason: _____ (**3**)

2. What feature does a streamlined object have? Give one example of a streamlined object. (**6**)

   _____

   _____

3. A helicopter landing pod has been added to a hospital in a residential area. Name one cost and one benefit. (**8**)

   Cost: _____

        _____

        _____

   Benefit: _____

        _____

        _____

        _____

26

ISBN: 978-1-897457-78-8

My Record

Section A	8
Section B	10
Section C	29
Section D	27
Section E	26

Total

100

80-100

Great work! You really understand your science stuff! Research your favourite science topics at the library or on the Internet to find out more about the topics related to this section. Keep challenging yourself to learn more!

60-79

Good work! You understand some basic concepts, but try reading through the units again to see whether you can master the material! Go over the questions that you had trouble with to make sure you know the correct answers.

below 60

You can do much better! Try reading over the units again. Ask your parents or teachers any questions you might have. Once you feel confident that you know the material, try the review again. Science is exciting, so don't give up!

ISBN: 978-1-897457-78-8

The Aeronautical Engineer

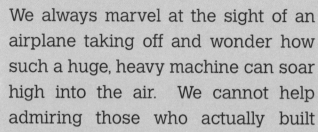

We always marvel at the sight of an airplane taking off and wonder how such a huge, heavy machine can soar high into the air. We cannot help admiring those who actually built these flying machines – the aeronautical engineers.

The first aeronautical engineers turned out to be two American brothers, Orville and Wilbur Wright. The Wright brothers are credited with inventing and building the world's first airplane and making the first controlled, powered, and sustained human flight on December 17, 1903. They later developed their flying machine into the first practical fixed-wing aircraft.

The Wright brothers gained the mechanical skills essential for their success by working for years in their shop with bicycles, motors, and other machinery. In fact, their bicycle shop employee, Charlie Taylor, took part in building their first aircraft engine.

Therefore, if you have a knack for machinery, you may make a great aeronautical engineer.

ISBN: 978-1-897457-78-8

Cool Science Facts

Jamen, keep holding the "tent".

1 How can we keep a structure from collapsing without using any columns or cables?

2 Why are some balls bouncier than others?

3 Solid tires do not flatten like air-filled tires do. Why do people still prefer air-filled tires?

4 Do springs have to be coils?

5 Hydrogen is lighter than helium. Why is hydrogen not used in balloons instead?

I'm a spring, too. Let's play together.

Find the answers on the next page.

ISBN: 978-1-897457-78-8

Cool Science Facts

1 We can support a structure with air. The dome stadium used by the Ontario Soccer Association is an air-supported dome structure. Air blowers attached to the structure blow air into it. Since the moving air inside the dome has greater air pressure than the outside, the fabric of the structure gets supported by the air and is pushed up. This inflates the stadium and gives it the dome shape.

2 In order to be bouncy, balls have to be made of elastic materials. When a ball hits the ground, it will deform, and this is when the ball stores the most potential energy for bouncing back. A ball that is more elastic allows it to store more potential energy when it is hit; hence, it will release more kinetic energy and be bouncier. Conversely, a ball that is less elastic stores less potential energy, so it is less bouncy.

ISBN: 978-1-897457-78-8

3 Air-filled tires can conform themselves to surfaces, and this provides maximum contact for traction. When air-filled tires run over small objects, such as rocks, the air acts as a shock absorber to reduce vibrations. Solid tires are not able to absorb bumps; they skip and lift up instead. Hence, people find it more comfortable to ride on cars with air-filled tires. Solid tires, however, are much more resistant to wear and tear. This makes them good for light industrial and household use, such as in forklifts and wheelbarrows, because they have high resistance to puncture damage.

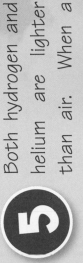

5 Both hydrogen and helium are lighter than air. When a balloon is filled with either gas, the air will push the balloon up. However, hydrogen is highly flammable, so it is not used in balloons.

4 Springs are not necessarily coils. Even a flat board, such as a diving board, will make a spring. A spring is something that returns to its original shape when it is no longer pushed or pulled.

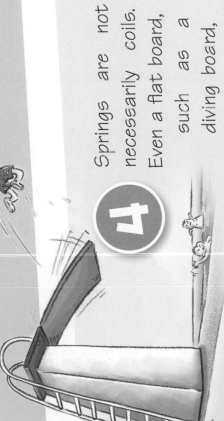

ISBN: 978-1-897457-78-8

ISBN: 978-1-897457-78-8

Section 3

Understanding Matter and Energy

ISBN: 978-1-897457-78-8

1 Current and Static Electricity

Electricity is part of our everyday lives. Current electricity is useful for powering technology at home, at school, and even outside. Static electricity is a natural phenomenon that happens without our control. In this unit, you will examine both kinds of electricity.

After completing this unit, you will

- know the difference between static and current electricity.

- know the effects of static electricity.

- know the difference between electricity from sockets and electricity from batteries.

Teddy, do you like your new hairstyle?

static electricity

TEDDY

DOGS

vocabulary

phenomenon: a natural event we perceive with our senses

stationary: still

phenomenon: lightning

ISBN: 978-1-897457-78-8

Have you ever seen lightning bolts darting down from the sky? Have you ever tried to toast a slice of bread with a toaster? If you have, you have some idea of the power of electricity. Humans are not the only ones that use electricity. Electric eels produce electricity in their bodies to repel their predators or kill their prey. The electric eel is one of the few animals on Earth that can make, store, and discharge electricity. An electric eel can produce an electric charge strong enough to injure a human!

A. Fill in the blanks to complete the descriptions. Then match the descriptions with the correct examples.

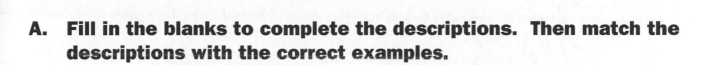

flow   static   contact   current

Types of Electricity

• _____ electricity:

   e.g. _____ , _____

   a stationary electric charge that builds up on a material due to its _____ with another material

• _____ electricity:

   e.g. _____ , _____

   a _____ of electric charge, which can be transformed into heat, light, and motion energy

A

B

C

D

B.   Fill in the blanks to complete the description of static electricity. Then draw the missing charges in the circles to illustrate static electricity.

Most objects have an 1._____ number of positive (+) and 2._____ (–) charges. If one object has an extra negative charge, it will stick to the 3._____ charge of another object. This is called **static** electricity.

> positive
>
> negative
>
> equal

An Example of Static Electricity
Rubbing a Balloon on a Woollen Sweater

□ : = / > / <

4.

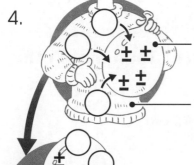

No. of (+) charges □ No. of (–) charges

Rubbing causes negative charges on the sweater to jump onto the _____ .

No. of (+) charges □ No. of (–) charges

The extra negative charges are attracted to the _____ charges on the wall. This attraction makes the balloon _____ .

C.   Label the pictures to show how we recognize static electricity.

A see a spark

B hear a crackle

C feel a shock

D materials stick together

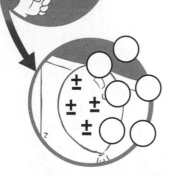

ISBN: 978-1-897457-78-8

D. Read the paragraph. Then describe each kind of electricity and provide examples of your own.

We get electricity from power plants through the sockets in our houses. This electricity is very powerful and does not run out. With it, we can power toasters, vacuums, ovens, and microwaves. This electricity, though, is not portable. It is also dangerous if we touch it because it can give us an electric shock that can hurt or even kill us. Batteries do not have the same disadvantages. They produce electricity from chemicals, which are stored inside them. They power cellphones, portable music players, and flashlights. They are small and portable, but compared to electricity from power plants, electricity from batteries is not very powerful.

I need some batteries for my toy cars.

1. Electricity comes from: _____

    Advantage: _____

    Disadvantage: _____

    Things that it powers: _____ , _____ , _____
                                               my example

2. Electricity comes from: _____

    Advantage: _____

    Disadvantage: _____

    Things that it powers: _____ , _____ , _____
                                               my example

2 Simple Electrical Circuits

Current electricity happens when electrical charges move through a system of parts called a circuit. In this unit, you will see how a simple circuit is constructed, and how it appears in a circuit diagram.

light bulb

Circuit Diagram

wire

wire

battery

After completing this unit, you will

- understand the difference between an open circuit and a closed circuit.

- understand the role of the components in a simple circuit.

an open circuit

a closed circuit

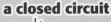

Vocabulary

circuit: a system of parts that allows electricity to flow

circuit diagram: a drawing of a circuit using symbols for its parts

open circuit: a circuit that does not function because there is a disruption in the electron flow

closed circuit: a circuit that functions because the electron flow is uninterrupted

ISBN: 978-1-897457-78-8

Universal symbols allow people to understand electrical circuit diagrams no matter where they live or what language they speak. This is not unique to electricity. The science of chemistry uses symbols to represent the elements. In our everyday lives, we use universal street signs and hazard symbols. Can you think of other areas that use universal symbols?

street sign

electrical circuit symbol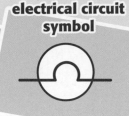

chemistry symbol

H_2O
(water)

hazard symbol

A. Fill in the blanks with the given words. Then label the terminals of the battery and draw the missing arrows to complete the diagram.

A circuit is a path along which 1._____ move. From the power source, such as a 2._____, the electrons flow along the path to the 3._____ it powers and back to the energy source again.

closed
electrons
battery
device

Electrons flow from the **negative** terminal to the **positive** terminal provided that the circuit is 4._____ .

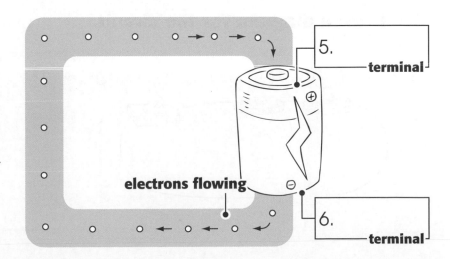

electrons flowing

5.

terminal

6.

terminal

B. Copy the universal symbols for the objects in a circuit. Then decide whether each circuit is "open" or "closed".

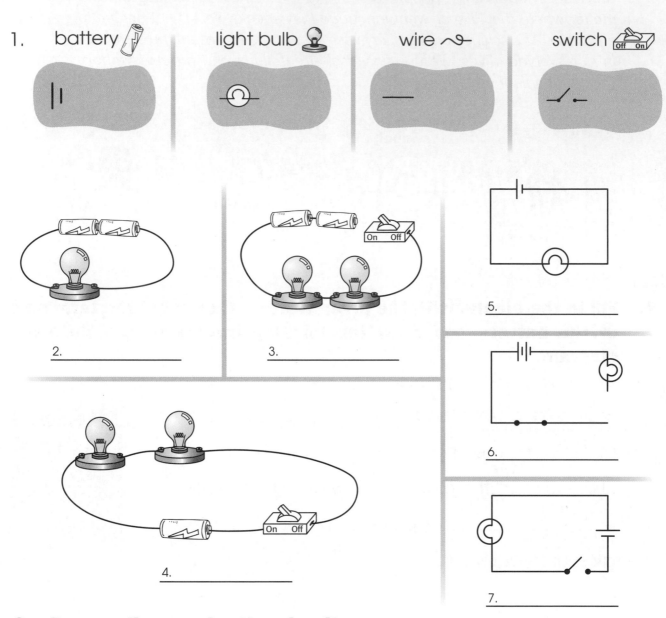

1. battery   light bulb   wire   switch

2. _____

3. _____

4. _____

5. _____

6. _____

7. _____

C. Draw a diagram for the circuit.

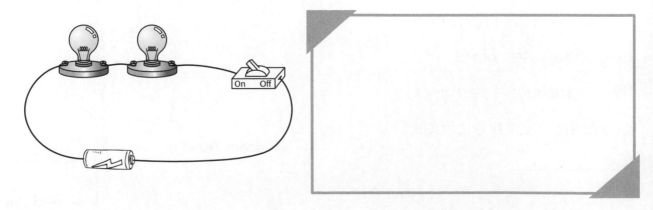

ISBN: 978-1-897457-78-8

D. Read the paragraph. Then answer the questions.

You have a simple electrical circuit as shown on the right. Imagine the light bulb is about as bright as your bedside lamp. Now add a second light bulb to your circuit. The two light bulbs are dimmer than the single light bulb of the original circuit. Now remove one light bulb and add one more battery. The single light bulb is much brighter than the light bulb of the original circuit.

original circuit

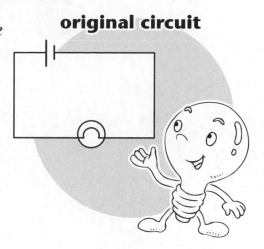

1. Describe the brightness of the light bulbs in the circuits below compared to the light bulb in the original circuit.

a.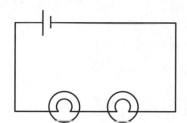

   brightness: _____

b.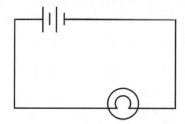

   brightness: _____

2. Draw a diagram for the circuit below. Then compare the brightness of the light bulbs with that of the original one by checking the correct answer.

schematic

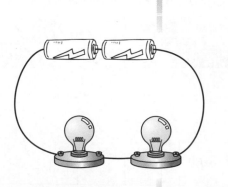

brightness
(compared to the original)

(A) dimmer

(B) brighter

(C) about the same

ISBN: 978-1-897457-78-8

3 Parallel and Series Circuits

Have you ever plugged in a set of patio lights to find that none of them lit up? The set is probably a series circuit. However, if your set allows other lights to stay lit when one is burned out, then it is a parallel circuit. In this unit, you will study series and parallel circuits.

Daddy, can you see that the other lights are working even though two lights are burned out? The chandelier must be a parallel circuit.

After completing this unit, you will

- understand how parallel and series circuits work and how they are different from each other.

Vocabulary

parallel: side by side

series: one after the other

Most lights work even though some are burned out.

 ISBN: 978-1-897457-78-8

Extension

There are many electrical circuits in your house. There are also many things that can keep you safe from the electrical currents running through them. In your house, electrical wires, like the ones connecting a lamp to an outlet, are covered in plastic or rubber. Houses also have circuit breakers. A circuit breaker is a switch that breaks its circuit if the circuit becomes unsafe. Ask an adult to show you the circuit breaker panel in your house to see just how many circuits there are in your house.

A. Trace the dotted lines to complete the circuits. Then fill in the blanks.

keep	parallel	chain-like	one	series	stop	branches

1. S_____ Circuit

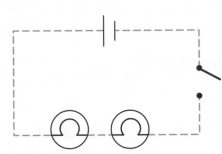

- allows electrons to follow only _____ path

- components are connected in a _____ order

- all the components _____ working if one component fails

2. P_____ Circuit

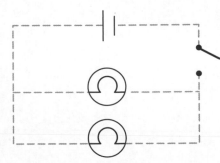

- different components are connected on different _____ of the wires

- the other components _____ working even if one fails

B. Decide whether each circuit is a "parallel" or "series" circuit and fill in the blanks.

1.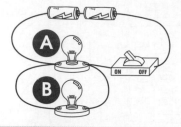

a _____ circuit

If **A** is burned out, **B** _____ working.
<u>stops/keeps</u>

2.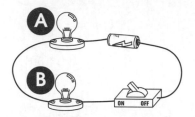

a _____ circuit

If **A** is burned out, **B** _____ working.
<u>stops/keeps</u>

3.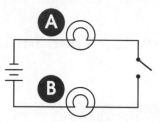

a _____ circuit

If **A** is burned out, **B** _____ working.
<u>stops/keeps</u>

4.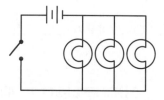

a _____ circuit

If one of the light bulbs is burned out, the

rest _____ working.
<u>stop/keep</u>

C. Draw one series circuit and one parallel circuit with each of the items provided.

- 1 battery (|l|)

- 1 switch (✓•)

- 3 light bulbs (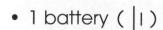)

Series	*Parallel*

ISBN: 978-1-897457-78-8

D. **Identify each circuit as a "series" or "parallel" circuit. Then match the circuits with the correct descriptions. Write the letters.**

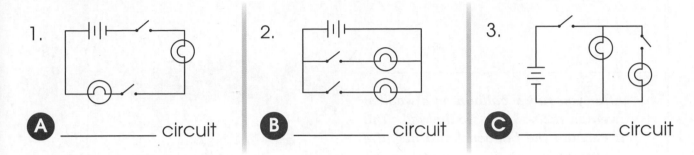

1.

A _____ circuit

2.

B _____ circuit

3.

C _____ circuit

4.

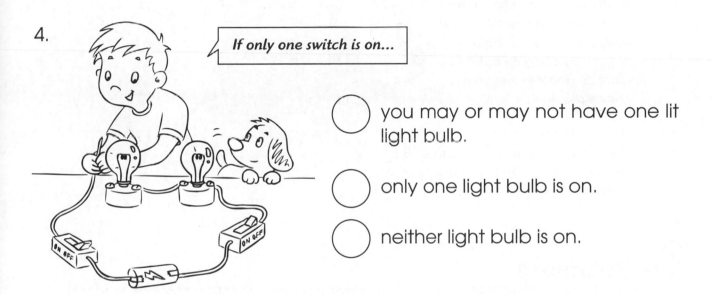

If only one switch is on...

◯ you may or may not have one lit light bulb.

◯ only one light bulb is on.

◯ neither light bulb is on.

E. **Draw the switches in the circuit diagrams so that they match the descriptions. Then colour the lit light bulbs yellow.**

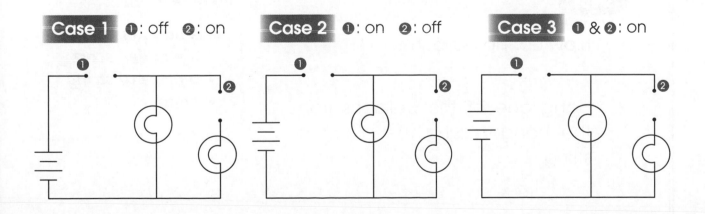

Case 1 ❶: off ❷: on   Case 2 ❶: on ❷: off   Case 3 ❶ & ❷: on

ISBN: 978-1-897457-78-8

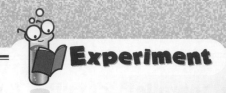

Experiment

Introduction

After you rub a balloon on a woollen sweater, it can "stick" to the wall. This is because the balloon has a negative electrostatic charge* and is attracted to the positive charges on the wall. What happens if you hold a negatively charged balloon close to another negatively charged object?

*electrostatic charge: a charge that builds up on an object if it has gained or lost electrons

Hypothesis

Circle one.

Two objects with like electrostatic charges   repel / attract each other.

Steps

1. Blow up the balloons.

2. Hang one of the balloons from the hanger using the piece of string.

Materials

- *2 balloons*
- *a woollen scarf*
- *a piece of string*
- *hanger*

ISBN: 978-1-897457-78-8

3. Rub the hanging balloon with the woollen scarf for about 15 seconds. Make sure you do not touch the balloon when you are done.

4. Rub the second balloon for 30 seconds while holding it by its end.

5. Bring the balloon that you are holding closer to the hanging balloon.

6. Observe and draw what happens.

Result

Observation:

_____

_____

Did the balloons repel or attract each other?

_____

Conclusion

The hypothesis was: _____

_____

My experiment _____ the hypothesis.

supported/did not support

4 Insulators and Conductors

Conductors are materials through which electrons can move easily. Insulators resist the movement of electrons. In this unit, you will see what kinds of materials conduct electricity and what kinds insulate against it.

> *Jenny, we should walk faster. Pool water conducts electricity, so we don't swim during a lightning storm.*

After completing this unit, you will

- know what insulators and conductors are.
- understand when and why each is used.

Vocabulary

impure water: water with impurities such as metals and minerals (almost all water is impure)

pure water: water with no impurities such as metals and minerals

pond: impure water

ISBN: 978-1-897457-78-8

Safety around electricity has a lot to do with knowing which materials electrons can flow through easily. Read the safety rules below to see how you can protect yourself from an electric shock.

Safety Rules

- Do not stand on a wet floor when using electrical appliances.

- Do not use electrical appliances with wet hands.

- Do not place electrical appliances near water.

Do you know what we should put away when we are using electricity?

Answer:

Answer: water

A. Fill in the blanks with the given words. Then give your own example.

conductor	insulator		
pure water	electrons	allows	tap water

1. An _____

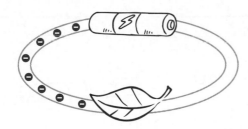

- a material that does not allow _____ to flow through it

- e.g. wood, air, fur, _____, and rubber

- my example: _____

2. A _____

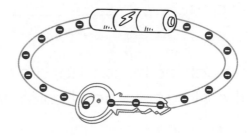

- a material that _____ electrons to flow through it

- e.g. aluminum, silver, gold, _____, and iron

- my example: _____

B. Look at the pictures and answer the questions.

1. Label each part with "insulator" or "conductor". Write the function of the insulators in the pictures.

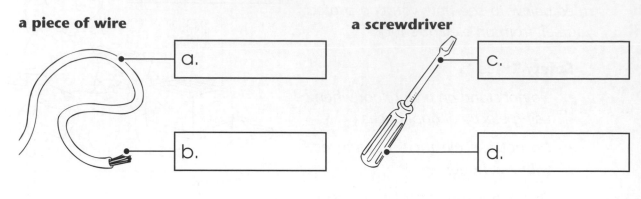

a piece of wire

a.

b.

a screwdriver

c.

d.

Function of insulators: _____

2. Circle the objects that are capable of making the circuit closed. Explain your choice.

Explain: _____

3. Check the liquids that are capable of making the circuit closed. Explain your choice.

Ⓐ rainwater   Ⓑ pure water

Ⓒ tap water   Ⓓ mineral water

Explain: _____

_____

ISBN: 978-1-897457-78-8

C. **Fill in the blanks to complete the paragraph and label the picture with the words in bold. Then answer the questions.**

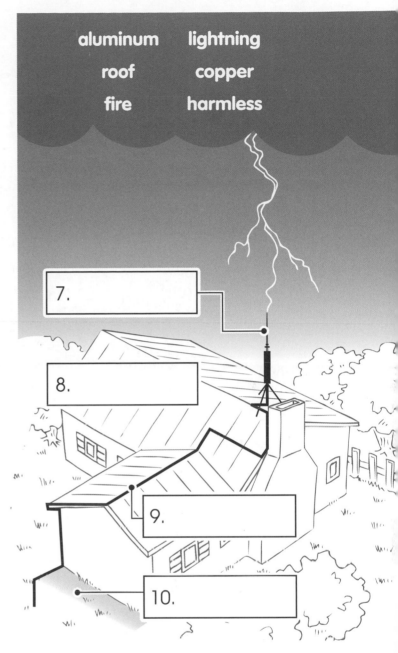

aluminum   lightning
roof   copper
fire   harmless

A **lightning rod** is a pointed metal rod mounted to a structure's 1._____ . Attached to it is a 2._____ or 3._____ **wire** that leads to the **ground**. The lightning rod and wire protect the **structure** during 4._____ storms by providing the lightning with a low resistance path to the ground where it is rendered 5._____ . If lightning were to strike the structure itself, it could hurt the people inside or cause a 6._____ .

7.

8.

9.

10.

11. Are the rod and wire conductors or insulators? Explain.

_____

_____

12. In Canada, we have a famous structure with a very tall lightning rod. What is it? Do you know how tall this structure is?

_____

5 Transformation of Energy

Electrical energy is available to us through the transformation of other forms of energy. We can also use electrical energy to make other forms of energy. In this unit, you will examine the different forms of energy that electrical energy is made from and turns into.

After completing this unit, you will

- understand that other forms of energy can be transformed into electrical energy.
- understand that electrical energy can be transformed into other forms of energy.

You know, the water from the falls generates more electricity!

No! Like I said, this wind farm generates more!

Vocabulary

transform: change

renewable: can be replaced

non-renewable: cannot be replaced

voltage: a force that makes electricity move

fossil fuels: non-renewable energy source

We get the energy we need to power our homes, businesses, schools, and vehicles from many different sources. There are two main kinds of sources: renewable and non-renewable. Renewable sources, such as wind, can be used without becoming depleted. Wind energy is renewable because no matter how much of it we use, it will never run out. Non-renewable sources, such as oil, do become depleted. The Earth cannot replace oil nearly as quickly as we use it, so we risk running out of it.

A. Fill in the blanks with the renewable energy sources. Then match them with the correct descriptions.

Renewable Energy Sources That Provide Electrical Energy:

sun   wind   tide
hot rock   moving water

_____ •

_____ •

• wind turbines are used to capture it

_____ •

• hydroelectric dams harness this energy

• solar panels are used to capture its rays

_____ •

• source of energy in coastal areas

_____ •

• heat is extracted from far beneath the ground; called geothermal energy

B. Fill in the blanks with the non-renewable energy sources.

**Non-renewable Energy Sources
That Provide Electrical Energy:**

oil   battery   coal
gas   nuclear

1. _____ : a compact energy source that starts as chemical energy

2. _____ energy: does not pollute the air, but we are unable to dispose of its waste safely

3. _____ , _____ , _____ : fossil fuels

C. Write the four types of energy that electricity can become. Then draw lines to match each type with the correct appliances.

mechanical   food   light
solar   sound   heat

Electrical Energy Becomes...

_____ energy •

_____ energy •

_____ energy •

_____ energy •

• lamp

• blender

• CD player

• ceiling fan

• oven

• sewing machine

ISBN: 978-1-897457-78-8

D. Read the paragraph. Use the words in bold to label the picture.

One common source of electrical energy in Ontario is moving water. How does that energy get into your house? It starts at the source of moving water, such as a fast-moving river or waterfall, where people have built a **hydroelectric dam.** *Once the energy has been harnessed by the dam, it travels through* **high-voltage power lines** *to a* **substation.** *Then it moves through* **low-voltage power lines** *and into your* **house.** *From a single point in the house, it is distributed to all of your* **electrical outlets.**

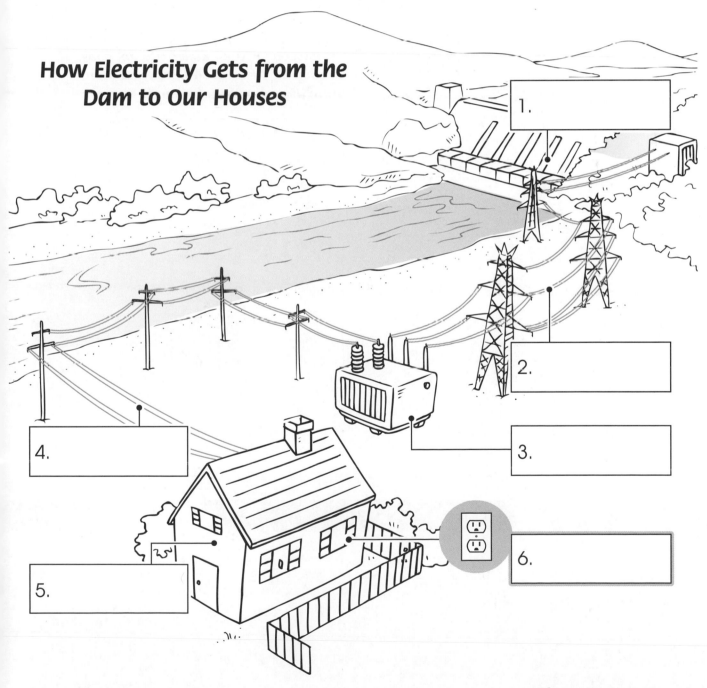

How Electricity Gets from the Dam to Our Houses

1.

2.

3.

4.

5.

6.

ISBN: 978-1-897457-78-8

6 Electricity and Us

The use of electricity has changed our society entirely. In this unit, you will look at some of these changes. You will also look at some of the damages its production does to the environment. Finally, you will examine some of the things you can do to reduce your use of electricity.

After completing this unit, you will

- understand the impact electricity has on society and the environment.
- understand that there are ways we can reduce electricity consumption.

The photocopier uses electricity to copy my document. It is much faster and more accurate than copying it by hand.

Vocabulary

consumption: the act of using

degrade: reduce in quality

degrading the land

ISBN: 978-1-897457-78-8

You have probably never known life without electricity, but not long ago people lived without it. What was life like then?

Then

Now

What else has changed? Do you think some things have stayed the same?

A. Fill in the blanks to show how electrical energy can damage the environment.

Costs of Using Electricity

land   air   habitats   toxic chemicals   land

1. Transmission lines and transformers use up tracts of _____ .

2. Solar-thermal plants produce power by using cells that are manufactured with _____ .

3. Hydroelectric dams wipe out _____ .

4. Fossil fuel extraction degrades the _____ .

5. Smoke from power plants pollutes the _____ .

ISBN: 978-1-897457-78-8

B. Check or circle the better choice. Then write two suggestions of your own.

To reduce electricity consumption, we can...

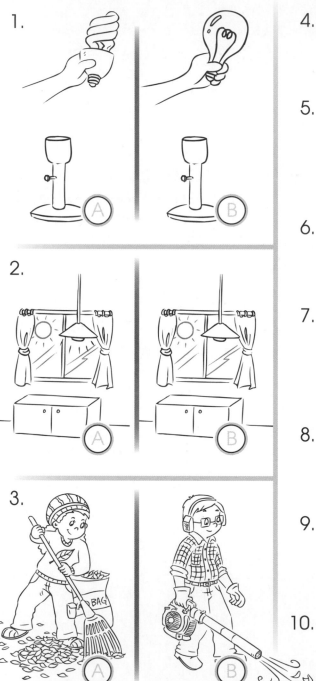

1.

2.

3.

4. choose **non-renewable / renewable** resources whenever possible.

5. make sure our homes are well **insulated / isolated** to prevent heat from escaping.

6. cool down with **air conditioning / ceiling fans** when it is hot.

7. turn **up / down** the heat at night or when we are not at home during winter.

8. turn appliances **on / off** when they are not being used.

9. _____

_____

10. _____

_____

ISBN: 978-1-897457-78-8

C. Fill in the blanks to complete the paragraph. Then answer the question.

heats	close	reach
hydroelectricity		surface
underground		heat
geothermal		Iceland
electricity		volcanoes

1. _____ energy comes from 2. _____ generated below the Earth's surface. This energy heats 3. _____ water, which is then piped to the 4. _____ where it is used for its heat or transformed into 5. _____ . Much of the world does not extensively use geothermal energy, as it can be difficult to 6. _____ . However, in some areas where the Earth's heat gets 7. _____ to the surface, it is easy to reach. 8. _____ is one such area. It is a country where heat constantly comes to the surface in the form of geysers, hot springs, and 9. _____ . Geothermal energy 10. _____ almost every building and supplies Iceland with a portion of its electricity. 11. _____ supplies the rest.

> Almost all of Iceland's electricity comes from renewable sources!

12. Is the man's comment true? Explain.

_____

_____

Introduction

Hot Water Tank Insulation

Since our use of electricity has consequences for the environment, we try to conserve energy and use as little electricity as possible. One way to do that is insulation. We put insulation in our walls, attics, and even around hot water tanks and pipes.

Hypothesis

This experiment tests three kinds of materials for insulation. Predict which will work best. Make your prediction the hypothesis.

Circle one.

Styrofoam / Cloth / Tissue is a great insulating material.

Materials

- *4 small, empty, and clean milk cartons*
- *4 ice cubes*
- *1 piece of styrofoam, cloth, and tissue*

Steps

1. Place one ice cube in each carton.

2. Place one kind of material around each ice cube. The one with no material will be your control.

  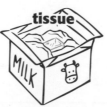 

to show you how the ice cube melts without any insulation

ISBN: 978-1-897457-78-8

3. Record the time you begin the experiment on the chart below.

4. Keep an eye on the ice cubes. Record the time when each one is fully melted.

> *You should have the ice cubes fully covered, so you'll have to peek beneath the material to check them.*

Start at

	Time Melted			
	Styrofoam	**Cloth**	**Tissue**	**Control**

Result

1. How long did it take each ice cube to melt?

    Styrofoam: _____   Cloth: _____

    Tissue: _____   Control: _____

2. Which material insulated its ice cube best?

    _____

Conclusion

The hypothesis was: _____

_____

My experiment _____ the hypothesis.
            supported/did not support

Try to complete this review in **30 minutes**.

30minutes

This review consists of five sections, from A to E. The marks for each question are shown in parentheses. The circle at the bottom right corner is for the marks you get in each section. An overall record is on the last page of the review.

A. Write T for true and F for false.

1. Electrical energy can be transformed into solar energy. **(2)** _____

2. When an object carries no charge, it has an equal number of negative and positive charges. **(2)** _____

3.

   Lake water is a good insulator. **(2)**

   _____

4. If a light bulb is out in a series circuit, none of the components works. **(2)**

   _____

8

ISBN: 978-1-897457-78-8

B. Do the matching.

1.
(2)

2.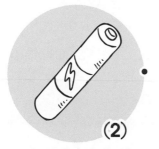
(2)

- represents a light bulb in a circuit diagram

- easily gains negative charges

3.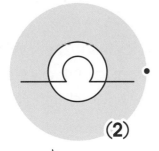
(2)

- a lightning rod

- geothermal energy escapes the Earth here

4.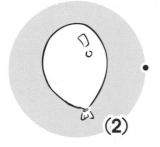
(2)

- portable device that transforms chemical energy into electrical energy

5.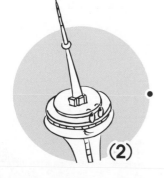
(2)

ISBN: 978-1-897457-78-8

10

C. Answer the questions.

1. Use the picture clues to name and write about two kinds of electricity. Then give an example of each.

a.

_____ **(1)** electricity

Description:

_____

_____

_____

_____ **(4)**

Example: _____ **(2)**

b.

_____ **(1)** electricity

Description:

_____

_____

_____

_____ **(4)**

Example: _____ **(2)**

2. After rubbing a plastic ruler on your hair, your hair looks frizzy. What has happened? Explain your answer using the concept of static electricity. Draw charges in the picture to illustrate your idea. **(8)**

before rubbing   **after rubbing**

_____

_____

_____

_____

_____

ISBN: 978-1-897457-78-8

D. Draw the specified circuits with the given components. Then answer the questions.

1. **a series circuit**: a switch, 2 batteries, 2 light bulbs, 4 wires

(6)

One light bulb is burned out. If the switch is on, does the other light bulb work?

_____ (3)

2. **a parallel circuit**: a switch, 2 batteries, 2 light bulbs, 5 wires

(6)

One light bulb is burned out. If the switch is on, does the other light bulb work?

_____ (3)

3. **a closed circuit**: a switch, a battery, 1 light bulb, 3 wires

(6)

Circle the items that can be used to replace the switch so that the circuit remains closed. (6)

| nail | straw | metal fork |
| rock | key | pure water |

4. Why do you think the circled items can close the circuit?

_____ (4)

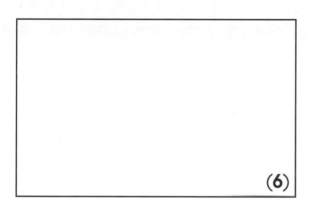

ISBN: 978-1-897457-78-8

34

E. **Give two examples of renewable and non-renewable sources of electricity. Name two different kinds of energy that electrical energy can become and give an example of each. Then answer the questions.**

1.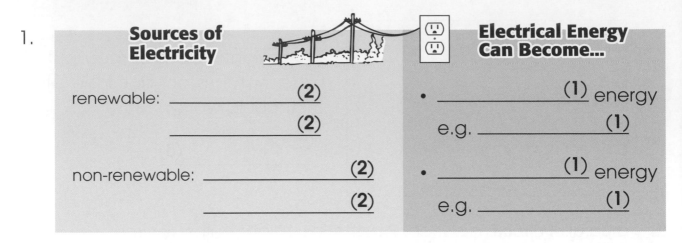

Sources of Electricity	Electrical Energy Can Become...
renewable: _____ **(2)**	• _____ **(1)** energy
_____ **(2)**	e.g. _____ **(1)**
non-renewable: _____ **(2)**	• _____ **(1)** energy
_____ **(2)**	e.g. _____ **(1)**

2. Does the use of electrical energy damage the environment? If yes, give two examples.

   _____

   _____

   _____ **(4)**

3. Describe the things people build to capture wind for generating electricity.

   _____

   _____ **(4)**

4. Suggest two ways Anya can reduce her energy consumption.

   Before I go to bed, I turn off my TV, turn on my bedside lamp, and turn up the heat.

   _____

   _____

   _____

   _____ **(6)**

26

ISBN: 978-1-897457-78-8

My Record

Section A	8
Section B	10
Section C	22
Section D	34
Section E	26

Total

100

80-100

Great work! You really understand your science stuff! Research your favourite science topics at the library or on the Internet to find out more about the topics related to this section. Keep challenging yourself to learn more!

60-79

Good work! You understand some basic concepts, but try reading through the units again to see whether you can master the material! Go over the questions that you had trouble with to make sure you know the correct answers.

below 60

You can do much better! Try reading over the units again. Ask your parents or teachers any questions you might have. Once you feel confident that you know the material, try the review again. Science is exciting, so don't give up!

ISBN: 978-1-897457-78-8

The Electrical Engineer

Electricity has been a subject of scientific interest since the early 17th century. William Gilbert is believed to be the first electrical engineer. He designed a device that could detect the presence of statically charged objects. In 1775, another electrical engineer Alessandro Volta made a device that produced a static electric charge, and by 1800, he developed the voltaic pile, an early form of the electric battery.

Electrical engineers are scientists who know how to put electricity into good use. They have contributed to the development of a wide range of technologies. They design, develop, test, and supervise the use of electrical systems and electronic devices. For example, they may work on the design of telecommunication systems, the operation of electric power stations, the lighting and wiring of buildings, the design of household appliances, or the electrical control of machinery.

Without electrical engineers, we would not have been able to enjoy the comfort and convenience of modern life that depends so much on electricity.

ISBN: 978-1-897457-78-8

Cool Science Facts

ISBN: 978-1-897457-78-8

1 What is inside a battery? How does a battery work?

2 How do we turn animal waste and organic materials into electricity?

3 Apart from us, what animal knows how to use electricity?

4 How do we remove scrap metal easily with the help of electricity?

Find the answers on the next page.

Cool Science Facts

1 A battery is made up of three major parts – a positive terminal, a negative terminal, and a chemical paste that separates the terminals. When a battery is connected to a circuit, chemical reactions start to take place inside the battery. This produces electrons, which flow from the negative terminal, light up the light bulb, and return to the battery through the positive terminal. Meanwhile, new electrons are produced. The process is repeated again and again. The chemical degrades gradually, and when the chemical can no longer make any more electricity, the battery "dies".

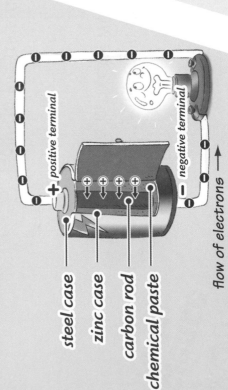

steel case
zinc case
carbon rod
chemical paste

positive terminal

negative terminal

flow of electrons →

2 When organic materials and animal waste are mixed with water, methane gas (a form of natural gas) is produced. The methane gas is then piped to a power plant to produce electricity.

This way of producing electricity reduces the amount of waste going to landfills and is more environmental-friendly than burning fossil fuels which produces lots of pollutants that harm the environment.

Power Plant

methane

ISBN: 978-1-897457-78-8

4 An electromagnet can be used for moving heavy metal objects from one place to another. When the operator switches on the electricity, a large iron disc that is attached to a crane becomes a magnet. When this disc is lowered, it attracts and grabs the scrap metal out from a pile. When the machine is switched off, the scrap metal falls off the disc. This way, large amounts of scrap metal can be sorted out easily.

3 Electric eels are able to make, store, and discharge electricity. The low intensity charges emitted by an eel range from 5 to 10 V, and the high intensity charges range from 450 to 650 V, which is about five times the power of a standard wall socket! The bodies of these special creatures contain electric organs with about 6000 specialized cells that store power like tiny batteries. When an electric eel is threatened or when it attacks prey, the cells will discharge a high voltage. Since they have poor eyesight, they emit a lower voltage to navigate and locate prey.

 ISBN: 978-1-897457-78-8

ISBN: 978-1-897457-78-8

Understanding
Earth and Space
Systems

ISBN: 978-1-897457-78-8

1 The Solar System

Our solar system is made up of many different bodies, from small pieces of dust to large planets. The planets, including the Earth, travel around the sun in their orbits. In this unit, you will identify the major bodies that make up the solar system.

After completing this unit, you will

- be able to name the bodies in the solar system, including the planets.

- understand that different bodies in the solar system are made up of different substances and have different orbital paths.

Vocabulary

planet: a large body with an elliptical orbit around the sun

elliptical: shaped like an oval

orbit: path around an object

solar: related to the sun

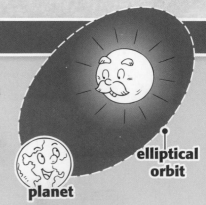

elliptical orbit

planet

ISBN: 978-1-897457-78-8

The sun provides us with heat, light, and energy. Without the sun, the Earth would be a dark, cold world with no life on it. Do you know what the sun is? Take a look at the model of the sun to see how amazing it is.

core: the hottest part of the sun; produces energy

radiation zone: the zone which emits radiation to transmit energy

convection zone: the circulating gases in this zone help transmit energy

A. Fill in the blanks with the words in the diagram.

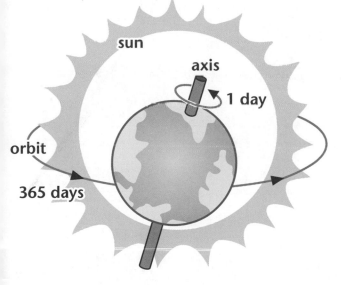

1. The Earth rotates on its _____ in a counter-clockwise direction.

2. It takes the Earth _____ to complete one full rotation.

3. All planets in the solar system revolve around the _____.

4. The Earth revolves around the sun in an elliptical _____.

5. It takes the Earth about _____ to complete one revolution around the sun.

B. Read the clues and use the words in bold to complete the diagram. Then fill in the blanks with the given words.

- **Jupiter** is the largest planet and **Mercury** is the smallest.
- **Mars** is the fourth planet from the sun.
- The **asteroid belt** lies between the orbits of Mars and Jupiter.
- **Saturn** has the most spectacular ring system.
- **Neptune** is the farthest planet from the sun and **Uranus** is the closest planet to Neptune.

outer
inner
rocky
gaseous
reddish
Venus

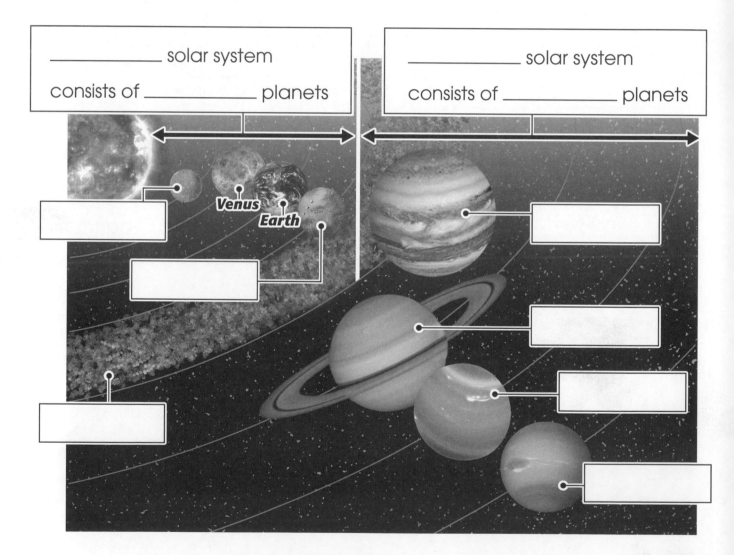

_____ solar system consists of _____ planets

_____ solar system consists of _____ planets

Venus

Earth

1. _____ is the hottest planet.

2. Mars appears _____ because there is iron oxide in its soil.

ISBN: 978-1-897457-78-8

C. Read the paragraph. Then label the diagram with the words in bold and answer the questions.

*Besides planets and asteroids, there are other bodies travelling in the solar system. A **meteoroid** is a solid body smaller than an asteroid floating in interplanetary space*. It can be as small as a dust particle. When such a body enters the Earth's atmosphere, it is called a **meteor**. It burns with a bright streak through the atmosphere, and is often called a "shooting star". When this body survives the Earth's atmosphere and hits the Earth's surface, it is known as a **meteorite**. If a meteorite is large, it will cause great damage to the Earth. Some people believe that dinosaurs became extinct because a very large meteorite hit the Earth millions of years ago.*

*interplanetary space: the space within our solar system

space

1.

2.

atmosphere

3.

Earth

4. What is a meteoroid? Where can it be found?

_____

5. What is a shooting star?

_____

6. What damage do you think a large meteorite may cause to the Earth?

_____

2 Bodies in Motion

crescent moon

The movements of the Earth, the moon, and their relative positions to each other and to the sun affect what happens around us. In this unit, you will examine some of these effects, like the different phases of the moon, which we can see in our daily lives.

After completing this unit, you will

- understand the effects of the movements of the Earth and the moon.

- understand the effects of the relative positions of the Earth, the moon, and the sun.

Elsie, look how beautiful the crescent moon is! We cannot see it every day because it is only one of the phases in the lunar cycle.

Vocabulary

lunar: related to the moon

Milky Way Galaxy: the galaxy which contains our solar system

moon phase: a cyclically recurring form of the moon

Milky Way Galaxy

solar system

ISBN: 978-1-897457-78-8

Everything in the solar system is moving, and these movements have great effects in our daily lives. The Earth rotates on its axis and this gives us day and night. Its tilted axis gives us seasons as it revolves around the sun. The movement of the moon around the Earth results in solar and lunar eclipses.

Solar Eclipse

moon
Earth

The moon blocks the light of the sun and a shadow of the moon is cast on the Earth.

Lunar Eclipse

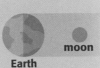

Earth
moon

The Earth throws a dark shadow across the moon.

Never look directly at the sun!

A. Fill in the blanks to complete the facts about the moon.

sun	27 days
Earth	craters
satellite	atmosphere

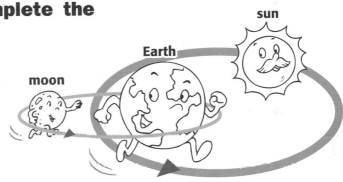

sun
Earth
moon

The Moon

1. The moon is the Earth's natural _____ .

2. The moon reflects light from the _____ .

3. The moon travels around the _____ .

4. It takes the moon about _____ to make a complete orbit around the Earth.

5. The moon has no _____ and it is covered with _____ .

B. **Read the paragraph. Then name the moon phases with the words in bold, colour the part of the moon we see from the Earth yellow, and fill in the blanks.**

*The phases of the moon depend on its position in relation to the sun and the Earth. The lunar cycle starts from a new moon, when there is complete darkness. It gradually becomes a **crescent moon**, and then grows fuller into a **first quarter**, when about half of the moon is seen. Then it becomes a **gibbous moon** (swollen on one side) before becoming a full moon. After that, it becomes a **gibbous moon** again and then enters the **last quarter** before changing into a **crescent moon**. Complete darkness follows and a new cycle begins.*

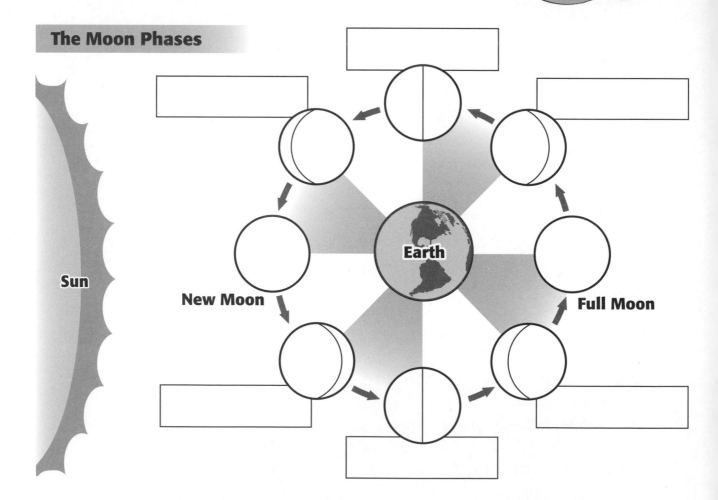

The Moon Phases

When the moon is more than half-lit, it is called a _____ moon.

When the moon is less than half-lit, it is called a _____ moon.

C. Read the paragraph. Then label the pictures and the diagram with the words in bold.

*Tides are the regular rising and falling of the sea level caused by gravitational pulls from the moon and the sun. When the moon is directly overhead, the gravitational pull is so strong that the water in the ocean is pulled towards the moon to create **high tide**. It is also high tide on the side of the Earth opposite the moon because as the Earth is pulled towards the moon, the water on that side is "left behind" as a bulge. At the same time, other locations experience **low tide**, where the water is pulled away. The highest tide takes place when the sun, the moon, and the Earth are aligned, because this is when the gravitational pulls on Earth are strongest.*

> Have you ever built a sandcastle at the beach? Did the high tide wash it away?

1. The Bay of Fundy

a.

b.

2. High and Low Tides

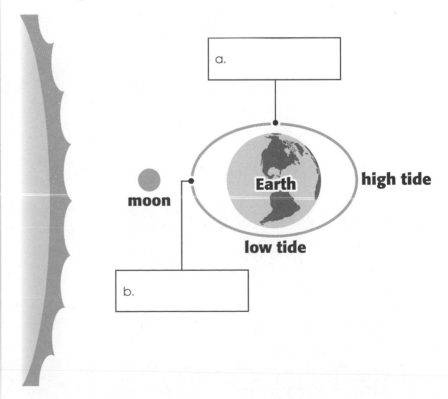

a.

moon

Earth

high tide

low tide

b.

3 Lights in the Sky

There are things in the night sky that emit their own light and others that appear as light to us but only reflect light. In this unit, you will examine what objects emit or reflect light, both on Earth and in the sky.

After completing this unit, you will

- understand that some objects emit their own light.
- understand that some objects that appear to emit their own light only reflect light.

Teddy, do you know that there are thousands of stars in the sky? What stars we can see depends on where we are on Earth and how bright the stars are.

Vocabulary

emit: give out

reflect: throw back

constellation: a group of stars forming a pattern as seen from the Earth

constellation

ISBN: 978-1-897457-78-8

All stars appear to be white at first glance. However, if you look at them more carefully or with binoculars, you will see that they actually come in a range of colours: blue, bluish white, white, yellowish white, yellow, orange, and red. The colours of stars are determined by their surface temperatures, with blue being the hottest and red being the coolest. Do you know what colour our sun, the only star in our solar system, is? With a surface temperature of 6000°C, the sun appears to be yellow.

A. Circle the correct words to complete the sentences. Then write whether each object "emits light" or "reflects light".

1. A star is a ball of **burning / sinking** gas. It gives out heat through great explosions. These explosions make the star so hot that it **floats / glows**. All stars **emit / detect** light.

2. The moon has a rocky body and emits **no / red** light. We can see the moon only because it **absorbs / reflects** sunlight.

The Moon

3.

The Sun

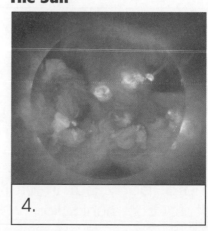

4.

B. Identify the objects in the night sky. Then write whether each object "emits" or "reflects" light.

satellite	meteor	Milky Way
moon	constellation	Jupiter

A _____ : _____ light

a rocky body that heats up once it has entered the Earth's atmosphere

B _____ : _____ light

a rocky body that orbits the Earth

C _____ : _____ light

the galaxy that our sun and solar system are parts of

D _____ : _____ light

a group of stars that form a pattern

E _____ : _____ light

the fifth planet from the sun

F _____ : _____ light

a metal body put in orbit around the Earth for communication

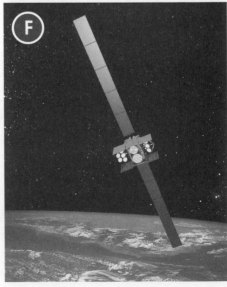

ISBN: 978-1-897457-78-8

C. Read the paragraph. Then circle the correct words to complete the facts about northern lights and answer the question.

Northern lights are like colourful light shows in the night sky. They are caused by particles that are shot out into space by the sun. When these particles reach the Earth, they are drawn into the magnetic field that surrounds the planet. They mix with different gases in the Earth's upper atmosphere and produce lights of vivid colours. Since the magnetic field is strongest in the North, that is where you can witness these spectacular light shows. Northern lights are not predictable, but it has been suggested that they are more common after major solar flares and sunspot activity on the sun's surface.

1. **Facts about Northern Lights:**

   • caused by **solar / water** particles

   • affected by the **electrical / magnetic** field of the Earth

   • are in **dull / bright** colours

   • take place **in space / near the North Pole**

   • are **predictable / unpredictable**

   • can especially be seen **before / after** major solar flares

2. There are southern lights that take place near the South Pole. Do you think they are as common as northern lights? Explain.

   _____

   _____

Introduction

Gravity is the force that keeps the Earth in its orbit around the sun and the moon in its orbit around the Earth. How much do you know about gravity? Did you know that weight is the force exerted by gravity on an object's mass? Does gravity pull a heavier object to the ground faster than a lighter object?

> *Will these two things of different weights fall to the ground at the same time?*

Hypothesis

Two objects of different weights   will / will not   fall to the ground at the same time.

Steps

1. Hold the sponge in one hand and the baseball in the other at the same height.

2. Let go of the sponge and the baseball at the same time, and record whether their landing times were the same or different.

Materials

- *a sponge*
- *a baseball*

ISBN: 978-1-897457-78-8

3. Repeat the first two steps at different heights, e.g. on different steps of a staircase.

| Drop them on the count of three. |

4. Record the results.

Result

Height (where the sponge and the baseball were dropped)	⚾ and 🧽 Landing Time: the same/different

Conclusion

The hypothesis was: _____

_____

My experiment _____ the hypothesis.

supported/did not support

4 Humans in Space

Scientific and technological advancement has allowed humans to venture out into space and even stay there for extended periods of time. In this unit, you will take a look at some examples of humans in space and examine the problems they need to overcome in order to live in space.

After completing this unit, you will

- be able to name some examples of humans in space.

- understand that humans must have their basic biological needs met in space.

- understand how technology helps humans adapt to life in space.

Do you think we can share our cookies with astronauts so that they can eat them in space?

Vocabulary

spacewalk: move outside a spacecraft in space

dehydrated: having water removed

atrophy: wasting away because of lack of use

dehydrated food

ISBN: 978-1-897457-78-8

International Space Station

The International Space Station (ISS) is one of the most exciting projects involving humans in space. ISS is an international space laboratory that conducts experiments. It is also an experiment in itself, in that astronauts live there for extended periods of time.

Size

72.8 m

108.5m

The ISS is in the final assembly stage. Once completed, the ISS will be slightly bigger than a soccer field and as heavy as 450 cars.

Weight

450 Cars

A. Fill in the blanks to complete the descriptions about these famous people in space.

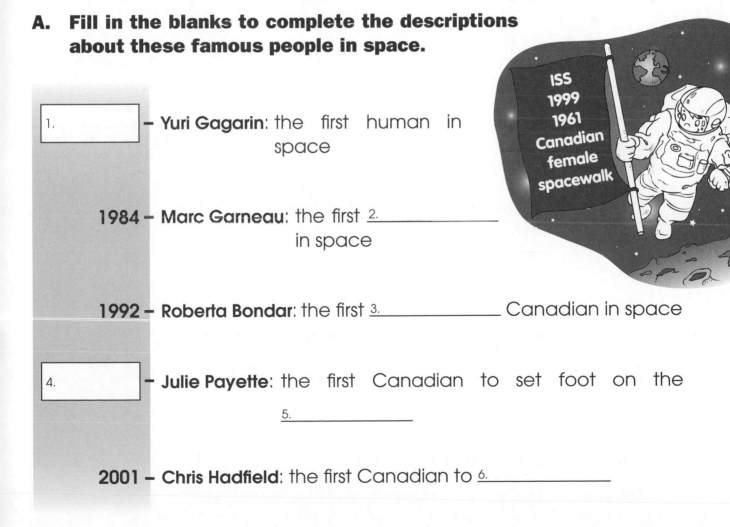

ISS
1999
1961
Canadian
female
spacewalk

1. _____ – **Yuri Gagarin**: the first human in space

1984 – **Marc Garneau**: the first 2._____ in space

1992 – **Roberta Bondar**: the first 3._____ Canadian in space

4. _____ – **Julie Payette**: the first Canadian to set foot on the 5._____

2001 – **Chris Hadfield**: the first Canadian to 6._____

ISBN: 978-1-897457-78-8

B. Write the biological needs of human beings. Then write the solutions to the problems associated with living in space.

Solutions

Biological Needs

- **food**
- **water**
- **exercise**
- **air**
- **hygiene**

- recycling used water, including water vapour from exhaled air
- providing machines and setting schedules for exercise
- providing freeze-dried or dehydrated food that takes up less space
- providing personal urinal funnels with fans to suck air and waste into the commode
- developing technology that makes air from water

1. _____

Problem: little room for storage and easily goes bad

Solution: _____

2. _____

Problem: no air in space

Solution: _____

3. _____

Problem: not enough room to carry and store

Solution: _____

4. _____

Problem: muscle and bone atrophy due to lack of use

Solution: _____

5. _____

Problem: how to get rid of waste

Solution: _____

C. Read the paragraph. Then complete the information chart.

In 2001, Dennis Tito, an American engineer and multi-millionaire, became the world's first "space tourist". He paid the Russian government a fee to fly on its Soyuz spacecraft to the International Space Station, which is located in low Earth orbit. He stayed there for seven days and performed several scientific experiments. In 2009, Guy Laliberté, the founder of Cirque du Soleil, took an 11-day journey to the ISS, making him the first Canadian and the seventh private space tourist. Laliberté's mission was to raise awareness for the ONE DROP Foundation, a non-profit organization he founded to fight poverty and ensure that everyone has access to water.

Information on Space Tourists

1. **The First Space Tourist**

Name: _____

Nationality: _____

Background: _____

_____

Year of Journey: _____

Length of Journey: _____

Things He Did: _____

2. **The Seventh Space Tourist**

Name: _____

Nationality: _____

Background: _____

_____

Year of Journey: _____

Length of Journey: _____

Aim of His Trip: _____

5 Technology and Space

Technology is always changing and improving, and is becoming more and more accessible. In this unit, you will examine how technology has helped humans explore space, both from space and from the Earth.

After completing this unit, you will

- understand that technology allows us to explore space.
- understand how some technological devices aid in the viewing and exploration of space.

Jimmy, I've made the Hubble Space Telescope for you. You can use this telescope to see or take pictures of faraway galaxies.

Vocabulary

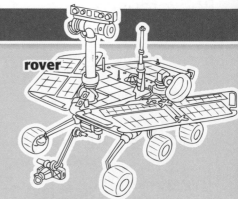

rover

rover: a vehicle that explores the surface of a planet

universe: all existing matter, energy, and space including the Earth, the solar system, and all galaxies

manned: having a human operator or crew on board

ISBN: 978-1-897457-78-8

For a long time many people believed that there was life on Mars. Now with the help of robotic spacecraft and small robotic vehicles called "rovers", which are controlled from the Earth, scientists have found no life on Mars. However, evidence of the presence of water in the form of polar ice caps and a small amount of water vapour in the Martian atmosphere suggests that there might be liquid water below these ice caps that may sustain life. Further advancement in technology will unearth more information about Mars and other planets in the solar system, and even objects farther away in the universe.

A. Match the technological devices with the descriptions. Write the letters.

A an orbiting, manned base for experiments and other operations in space

B gives a better view of objects in space from the Earth

C propels a spacecraft into space

D an unmanned spacecraft

E a manned spacecraft

space shuttle [1]

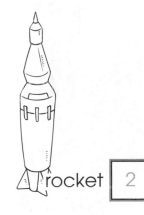

rocket [2]

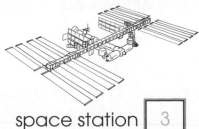

space station [3]

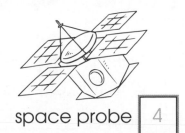

space probe [4]

telescope [5]

B. Name each technological device that allows us to see things in the sky. Then fill in the blanks to complete the descriptions.

planetarium telescope	universe constellations
binoculars Hubble Space Telescope	Saturn's rings moon's surface

1 _____

Its orbit outside the Earth's atmosphere allows clear views of the deepest parts of the _____ .

2 _____

Here we can view images of planets and _____ projected onto a dome-shaped ceiling.

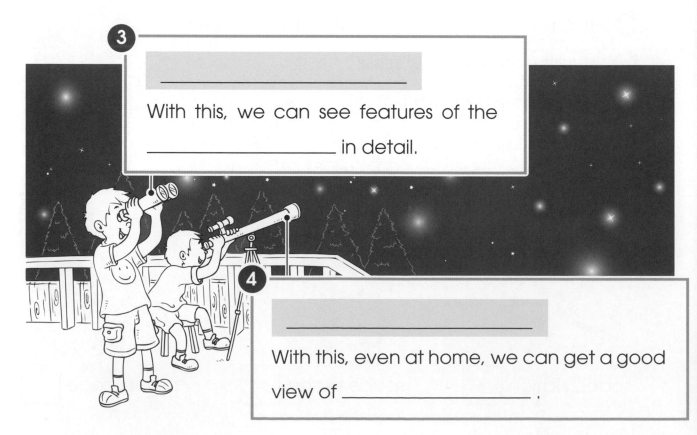

3 _____

With this, we can see features of the _____ in detail.

4 _____

With this, even at home, we can get a good view of _____ .

ISBN: 978-1-897457-78-8

C. Read the paragraph. Then check the picture showing the safe way to view a solar eclipse and answer the questions.

A solar eclipse occurs when the moon passes between the Earth and the sun and blocks out the sun's light as seen from some locations on Earth. Viewing a solar eclipse with the naked eye may cause eye damage or blindness. The safest way to view a solar eclipse is by using pinhole projection. Simply use two sheets of white cardboard and make a small hole in the centre of one of them. Standing with your back to the sun, hold the cardboard with the hole facing towards the eclipse. Place the other sheet on the ground to watch the image of the solar eclipse cast on it.

1.

2. What is a solar eclipse?

_____

_____

_____

_____

3. Why is it unsafe to view a solar eclipse with the naked eye?

_____

_____

_____

6 Space Exploration and Society

After completing this unit, you will

- understand that space exploration has both social costs and benefits.

- be able to name some jobs related to space exploration.

- understand the importance of space exploration to our society.

Space exploration is an extravagant excess of our society, but at the same time, it gives answers to questions humans have been asking since time began. In this unit, you will look at some of the costs and benefits of space exploration, as well as careers people have made out of it.

Our project is almost completed. This space shuttle is ready to be launched.

It's a really expensive project. I hope this mission will pay off.

Vocabulary

aerodynamic: designed to reduce the force of drag

aerospace: related to the Earth's atmosphere and to space

celestial: related to the sky or outer space

telecommunication: communication at a distance

telecommunication

ISBN: 978-1-897457-78-8

Human space exploration has both benefits and costs to society. It takes a lot of money to develop and manufacture the necessary technology for space programs. Some people think that this huge sum of money should be used to solve problems on Earth instead. However, have you noticed that many things we use now are actually by-products of space exploration programs? Below are some examples.

By-products of Space Exploration Programs:

- *better water purification system*
- *better weather forecasting*
- *aerodynamic swimsuit material for competitive swimmers*
- *improved shock absorption in running shoes*

shock-absorbing running shoes

A. Write the letters to identify the advantages and disadvantages of space exploration.

A It gives answers to questions about things beyond the Earth that humans have been asking since time began.

B Huge sums of money have been spent on developing technology for space programs.

C There are potential dangers for astronauts in space.

D It brings us new technology.

E It creates many jobs in the aerospace industry.

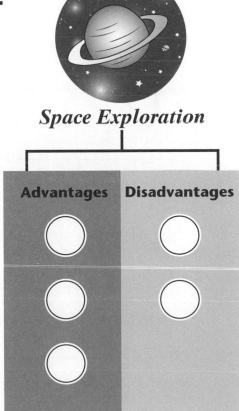

Space Exploration

B. **Name the job titles related to space exploration. Then complete the descriptions.**

astronomer	physical properties
aerospace engineer	pilot or crew member
astronaut	surface and interior processes
planetary geologist	satellites and spacecraft
astrophysicist	celestial bodies

Title

1

I am a scientist and I study planets, stars, and other _____ .

2. **Title**

- person trained to be the _____ of a spacecraft

3. **Title**

- someone who designs and builds _____ _____

4. **Title**

- someone who studies the _____ of planets, stars, and other celestial bodies

5. **Title**

- someone who studies the _____ _____ of celestial bodies other than the Earth in the solar system

 ISBN: 978-1-897457-78-8

C. Read the paragraph. Trace the dotted lines to show how people communicate through a satellite. Then write the functions of the three types of satellites and answer the question.

Without space exploration, life today would not have been the same. The many artificial satellites operating in Earth's orbit are the most obvious examples among all. Communications satellites make telecommunications around the world possible through the telephone, radio, and television. Navigation satellites provide us with positioning and navigation services. Weather satellites observe and monitor the Earth's weather and climate, and predict weather conditions. Can you imagine your life without these modern luxuries?

1. **Functions**

   communications satellites: _____

   navigation satellites: _____

   weather satellites: _____

2. Which type of satellite do you think affects today's society the most? Why?

   _____

   _____

Experiment

Introduction

Satellites are put into orbit by rockets, but once they are free from the rocket and circling the Earth, there is nothing to keep them there but gravity.

Let's do an experiment to show how satellites stay in orbit.

Do you need some tape?

Read through the experiment and choose a prediction.

1. A force will act on the water to keep it in the bucket, even when it is upside down.

2. The water in the bucket will spill all over me when the bucket is upside down.

Hypothesis

The hypothesis based on the prediction you chose:

_____

_____

Materials

- *a small bucket with a handle*
- *water*

ISBN: 978-1-897457-78-8

Steps

1. Fill the bucket half full with water.

2. Go to your backyard with the bucket. Keep a safe distance from any people or objects.

3. Holding the handle of the bucket and keeping your arm straight, swing the bucket quickly in complete circles.

Swing it faster, Jenny. The quick movement creates an inward force that pulls the water.

Result

Write what happened.

_____

_____

Conclusion

The hypothesis was: _____

_____

My experiment _____ the hypothesis.
   supported/did not support

Try to complete this review in **30 minutes**.

30 minutes

This review consists of five sections, from A to E. The marks for each question are shown in parentheses. The circle at the bottom right corner is for the marks you get in each section. An overall record is on the last page of the review.

A. Write T for true and F for false.

1. Roberta Bondar was the first female Canadian to set foot on the International Space Station. **(2)**

_____

2. An astrophysicist is a person who studies the physical properties of planets, stars, and other celestial bodies. **(2)**

_____

3.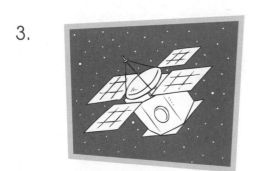

We can see a satellite in the night sky because of the lights on it. **(2)**

_____

4.

The International Space Station (ISS) is a manned base for experiments and other operations in space. **(2)**

_____

8

ISBN: 978-1-897457-78-8

B. Do the matching.

1.

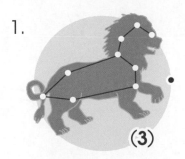

(3)

2.

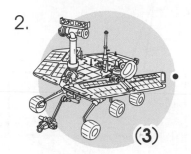

(3)

- the galaxy which contains our solar system

- a group of stars that form a pattern as seen from the Earth

3.

(3)

- orbiting outside the Earth's atmosphere to take clear pictures of faraway galaxies

4.

(3)

- makes telecommunications around the world possible

- a vehicle that explores the surface of a planet

5.

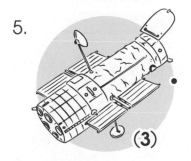

(3)

15

ISBN: 978-1-897457-78-8

C. Draw and name the missing planets in the solar system. Then label and shade the asteroid belt and answer the questions.

1.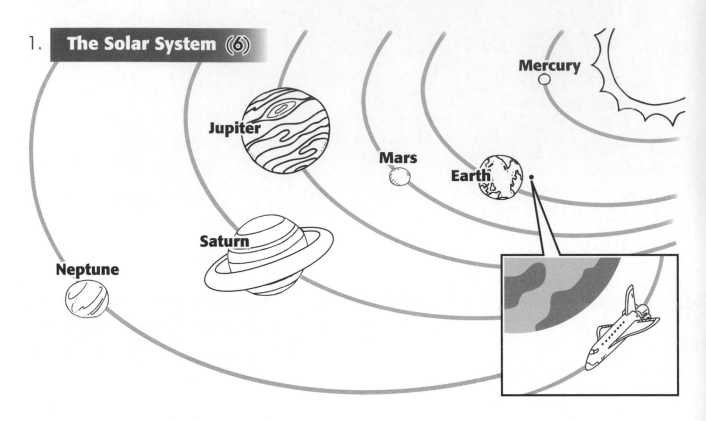

2. Name any two planets that are

   a. in the inner solar system. **(4)** _____

   b. in the outer solar system. **(4)** _____

   c. gaseous planets. **(4)** _____

3. Name the manned spacecraft that is shown in the box above. **(2)** _____

4. What do we call a scientist who is trained to be the pilot of a spacecraft? **(2)** _____

5. State one problem that humans face in space and the solution to this problem. **(6)**

   problem: _____

   solution: _____

28

ISBN: 978-1-897457-78-8

D. Name the moon phases in the diagram. Then answer the questions.

1. **Phases of the Moon** (8)

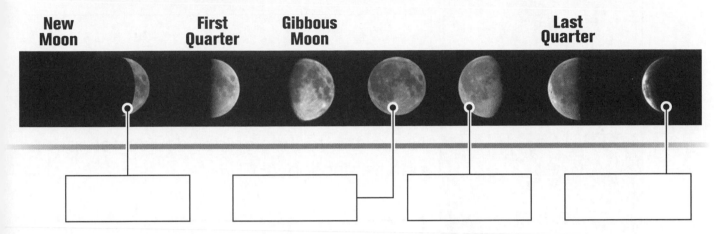

New Moon   First Quarter   Gibbous Moon   Last Quarter

```
┌──────────┐   ┌──────────┐   ┌──────────┐   ┌──────────┐
│          │   │          │   │          │   │          │
└──────────┘   └──────────┘   └──────────┘   └──────────┘
```

2. What is the moon called when it is more than half-lit? **(2)**

_____

3. How long does it take the moon to make a complete orbit around the Earth? **(2)**

_____

4. Does the moon emit light? If no, why can we see the moon? **(3)**

_____

5. Name the technological device that can be used on Earth to view the features of the moon's surface in detail. **(2)**

_____

6. What happens when the moon passes between the Earth and the sun, and the three of them are aligned? **(2)**

moon   Earth

_____

19

ISBN: 978-1-897457-78-8

E. Look at the pictures. Answer the questions.

1.

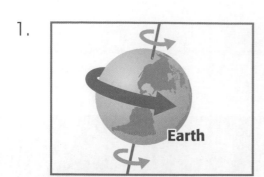

Write what the picture shows. **(6)**

_____

_____

_____

2.

Name this technological device for space and its function. **(6)**

_____

_____

3.

Give one advantage and one disadvantage of space exploration. **(6)**

_____

_____

_____

4.

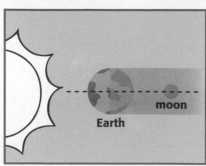

Does the moon have an atmosphere? What is it covered with? **(6)**

_____

_____

5.

Write what the picture shows. **(6)**

_____

_____

_____

30

ISBN: 978-1-897457-78-8

My Record

Section	
Section A	8
Section B	15
Section C	28
Section D	19
Section E	30

Total

100

80-100

Great work! You really understand your science stuff! Research your favourite science topics at the library or on the Internet to find out more about the topics related to this section. Keep challenging yourself to learn more!

60-79

Good work! You understand some basic concepts, but try reading through the units again to see whether you can master the material! Go over the questions that you had trouble with to make sure you know the correct answers.

below 60

You can do much better! Try reading over the units again. Ask your parents or teachers any questions you might have. Once you feel confident that you know the material, try the review again. Science is exciting, so don't give up!

The Recycling Plant Worker

When recyclable materials are collected from our bins, they go to a materials recovery facility (MRF – pronounced "merf"). There, recycling plant workers will have them recycled. First, they dump all the materials onto a conveyer belt, from which they remove the non-recyclable waste and sort the recyclables according to their type of material.

The rest of the recycling process is different for each type of material. Glass, for example, is chipped and then melted so that it can be made into new glass objects. Some recycling plants also offer bottle reclamation, in which bottles are sterilized for reuse. Plastic, metal, and paper are usually shredded for processing, while paper products are pulped into a slurry which can be made into paper again.

Recycling plant workers' jobs are meaningful because they turn waste to useful products and help conserve resources.

ISBN: 978-1-897457-78-8

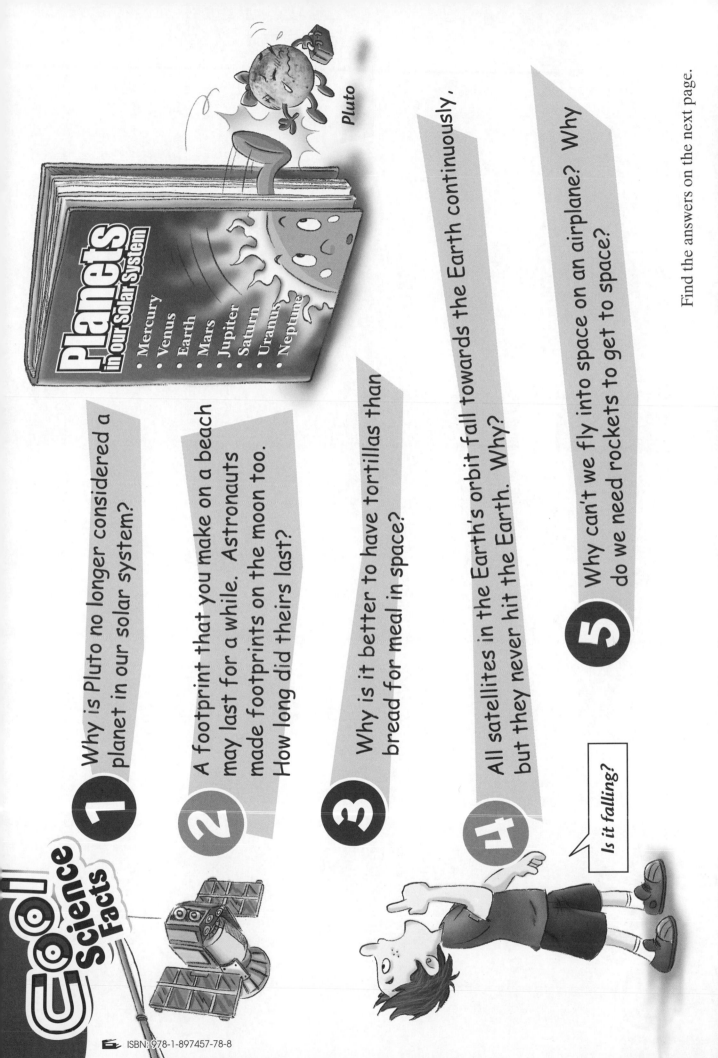

Cool Science Facts

Planets in our Solar System
- Mercury
- Venus
- Earth
- Mars
- Jupiter
- Saturn
- Uranus
- Neptune

Pluto

1. Why is Pluto no longer considered a planet in our solar system?

2. A footprint that you make on a beach may last for a while. Astronauts made footprints on the moon too. How long did theirs last?

3. Why is it better to have tortillas than bread for meal in space?

4. All satellites in the Earth's orbit fall towards the Earth continuously, but they never hit the Earth. Why?

Is it falling?

5. Why can't we fly into space on an airplane? Why do we need rockets to get to space?

Find the answers on the next page.

ISBN: 978-1-897457-78-8

Cool Science Facts

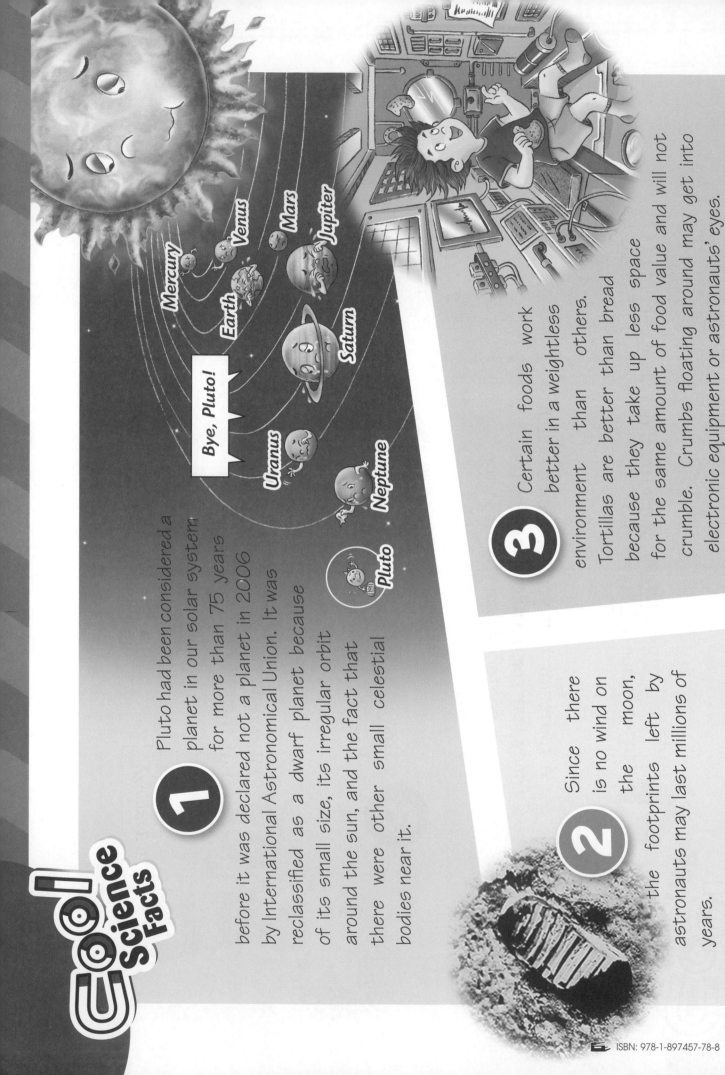

Mercury
Venus
Earth
Mars
Jupiter
Saturn
Uranus
Neptune
Pluto

Bye, Pluto!

1 Pluto had been considered a planet in our solar system for more than 75 years before it was declared not a planet in 2006 by International Astronomical Union. It was reclassified as a dwarf planet because of its small size, its irregular orbit around the sun, and the fact that there were other small celestial bodies near it.

2 Since there is no wind on the moon, the footprints left by astronauts may last millions of years.

3 Certain foods work better in a weightless environment than others. Tortillas are better than bread because they take up less space for the same amount of food value and will not crumble. Crumbs floating around may get into electronic equipment or astronauts' eyes.

ISBN: 978-1-897457-78-8

5

Airplanes are able to fly because air moving under their wings is strong enough to hold them up. Air gets thinner at a high altitude. Therefore, air is no longer able to hold an airplane up when the plane goes beyond a certain altitude. Rockets do not depend on air to lift them up. When a rocket is lit, it gives out large amount of hot gases, which force the rocket to blast off.

4

The gravitational force attracts us towards the centre of the Earth, so no matter where we stand on Earth, we do not fall into space.

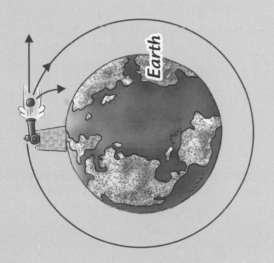

Imagine there is a cannon firing a cannonball in the diagram above. If the speed of the cannonball is too low, it will crash into the Earth due to the strong gravitational pull. If the speed is high enough, the cannonball will escape the gravitational attraction of the Earth. With the right speed, the cannonball will continuously fall towards the Earth, but never hit it. All satellites stay in the Earth's obit in the same way.

 ISBN: 978-1-897457-78-8

ISBN: 978-1-897457-78-8

Answers

ISBN: 978-1-897457-78-8

Section 1

1 Biodiversity

A. biological + diversity
   1. A   2. C

B.

A, C, B

C. 1. A   2. E   3. F   4. J
   5. B   6. I   7. G   8. C
   9. H   10. D

D. 1. threadsnake ; snake ; reptile ; 10 cm
   2. Charrier coffee ; plant ; naturally caffeine-free
   3. Satomi's pygmy seahorse ; seahorse ; fish ; 13.8 mm
   4. Tahina palm ; plant ; self-destructing
   5. Microbacterium hatanonis ; bacterium ; Japanese scientists ; able to live in extreme environments

2 Classification

A.

Five Kingdoms of Life

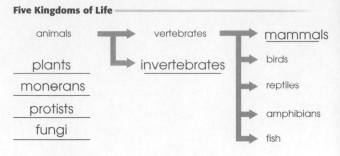

B. (Suggested examples)
   1. Birds ; e.g. swan
      feathers ; wings ; warm-blooded ; lay eggs on land
   2. Fish ; e.g. salmon
      fins ; lay eggs in water ; cold-blooded ; scales
   3. Reptiles ; e.g. turtle
      scales ; lay eggs on land ; cold-blooded
   4. Amphibians ; e.g. frog
      moist skin ; lay eggs in water ; cold-blooded
   5. Mammals ; e.g. cat
      warm-blooded ; hair or fur ; nurse young

C. 1. invertebrates 2. exoskeleton
   3. strong   4. three
   5. head   6. thorax
   7. abdomen   8. compound
   9. antennae   10. legs
  11. six   12. wings

D. 1. insects   2. largest
   3. mouthparts   4. antennae
   5. exoskeleton   6. non-flying wings
   7. Goliath Beetle ; 11 cm ; 100 g ; tropical forests of Africa ; tree sap, fruit, dead plant material, dung ; brown, white, and black
   8. Nanosellini ; 1 mm ; fungi ; fungal spores

ISBN: 978-1-897457-78-8

3 Biodiversity and Communities

A.

Biomes
Tundra
Grassland
Desert
Tropical Rainforest
Deciduous Forest
Coniferous Forest

- very little rainfall; cacti, lizards, and nocturnal animals
- fertile earth; grazing animals and their predators
- ice and permafrost; small plants and caribou
- trees that lose leaves in the winter; deer and songbirds
- warm temperatures, wet; many different species
- cool weather supporting evergreen trees; spruce and pine trees, beavers, and moose

B. 1. Biotic elements:
   birch trees ; pine trees ; mountain lion ; bobcat ; white-tailed deer ; mushrooms ; snowshoe hare
   Abiotic elements:
   cloud ; wind ; rock ; soil
   2. Biotic elements:
   caribou ; grass ; polar bear ; lemming ; Arctic fox ; dwarf plants
   Abiotic elements:
   snow ; ice ; mountain

C. 1. genes   2. alike
   3. Diversity   4. taste
   5. cook
   (Colour the apples.)
   6. (Suggested answers)
   Differences: size ; ear position ; colour and texture of fur
   Similarities: four legs ; long nose ; a tail ; fur
   7. (Individual answer)

D. 1. Temperate Rainforest ; coast of British Columbia
   Mountain Biome ; southern British Columbia and Alberta
   Grassland ; southern Alberta
   Tundra ; northern Canada
   Temperate Deciduous Forest ; southeastern Canada
   Boreal Forest ; south of the tundra

2. (Suggested examples)
   a. Boreal Forest ; 100 cm ; coniferous ; bears ; deer
   b. Temperate Deciduous Forest ; greatest ; deciduous ; oak ; wolves ; deer
   c. Tundra ; grasses and shrubs ; caribou

Experiment

(Possible experiment outcome)
Result: yes ; warm
Conclusion: Living things need specific conditions to grow well. ; supported

4 Biodiversity: Connections

A. A: producer
   B: consumer ; herbivore
   C: consumer ; carnivore
   D: consumer ; omnivore
   E: consumer ; herbivore
   F: decomposer

B. 1. rabbit, squirrel, grass, insect
   2. leaf, acorn
   3. (Suggested chains)
   a. grass ➡ deer ➡ cougar
   b. leaf ➡ rabbit ➡ hawk
   c. leaf ➡ insect ➡ fox

C. 1. A, C, D
   2a. eggs ; prey
   b. plants ; pollen

D. 1. Commensalism: Burdock relies on furry animals to disperse its seeds. Furry animals rarely notice.

2. Mutualism: A bear eats blackberries to fatten up for the winter. The bear disperses blackberry seeds.

3. Parasitism: The cuckoo lays its eggs in another bird's nest. That bird raises the cuckoo chicks at the expense of its own young.

5 Human Activities and Biodiversity

A. 1. botany   2. zoology
   3. evolution   4. conservation
   5. genetics

B. (Suggested examples)
   1. clothing ; silk scarf ; hemp jacket
   2. recreation ; skateboard ; zoo
   3. medicine ; traditional painkiller ; ginger (for stomachache)
   4. food ; tofu ; chicken
   5. household ; leather sofa ; cotton bedding

C. (Suggested answers)
   E ; A
   F ; C
   B ; D
   homeowner ; "Keep it forested so that my family has a place to explore."
   wilderness tour operator ; "Keep it forested so that I can keep my business running."

D. 1. Haida ; Canada's Pacific coast ; water, cedar and spruce forests, salmon ; houses, clothing, canoes (fishing), totem poles

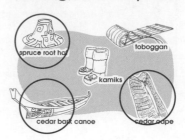

2. Inuit ; the Arctic ; caribou, seal, and walrus
   (Suggested examples)
   a. houses
   b. tools
   c. oil for cooking
   d. waterproof clothing

6 Biodiversity: Threats and Solutions

A. (Suggested answers)

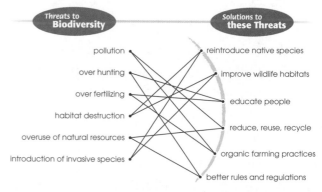

B. 1. special concern ; Blue Ash
   2. threatened ; Grey Fox
   3. endangered ; Whooping Crane
   4. extirpated ; Oregon Lupine
   5. extinct ; Labrador Duck

C. Law: A, D
   Education/Example: B, C, E, F

D. 1. largest land animal in North America ; up to 1000 kg ; meadows of Canada's boreal forest ; grasses, sedges, tree leaves, and tree bark

2. 200 000 ; decreasing ; over hunting
200 ; endangered ; Recovery ; protecting the wood bison and reintroducing it ; recovering
4000 ; threatened

3. (Individual answer)

Experiment

(Individual experiment outcome)

Review

A. 1. F   2. T
   3. F   4. T

B. 1.

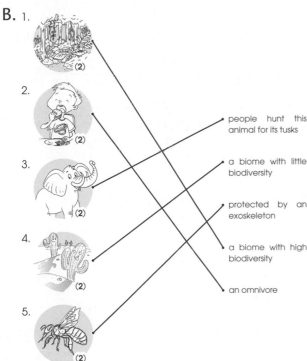

C. (Suggested characteristics and examples)
1. animals
2. plants
3. vertebrates
a. have moist skin
b. frog
c. lay eggs in water
d. goldfish
e. mammals
f. black bear
g. birds
h. Canada goose
i. reptiles
j. lay eggs on land
4. invertebrates
Insects: A, C, E
have exoskeletons ; have three body segments ; have three pairs of legs

D.
1.

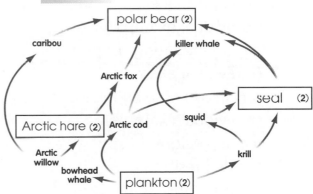

2. (Suggested examples)
Arctic fox ; Arctic hare ; Arctic willow

3. (Suggested answers)
ice ; cold temperature

4. This food web exists in the tundra.

5. (Suggested answer)
Humans extract natural resources.

ISBN: 978-1-897457-78-8

E. 1. B

2. It is mutualism because both organisms benefit from the relationship.

3a. The plant would be destroyed, and the moth would no longer have food for its larvae or a place to lay eggs.

b. They would be upset because it would damage this special relationship and also threaten biodiversity in general.

c. They would be happy because it would mean that they would have work.

Section 2

1 Properties of Air

A. 1. takes up space
(Individual example)

2. has an insulating property
(Individual example)

3. pushes on objects
(Individual example)

B. 1. more ; weight

2. slowly ; resists

3. warmth ; insulating

4. less ; rises ; heated

5. air ; space

6. compressed ; compressed

7. outside ; pushes

(Individual examples)

Air has weight.

Air resists things moving through it.

Air has an insulating property.

Air expands when heated.

Air takes up space.

Air can be compressed.

Air pushes on objects.

C. 1.

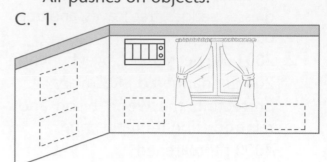

The air conditioner should be placed high up because cool air sinks and warm air rises.

2.

Heated air rises, so if you want to heat the whole space, the heater should be placed on the floor.

3. Cold air is heavy, so it will not leave the floor display freezer and can keep the food in it frozen.

2 Four Forces of Flight

A.

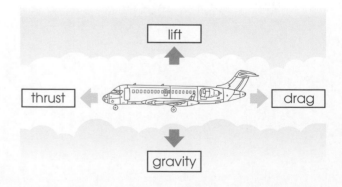

ISBN: 978-1-897457-78-8

B. 1.

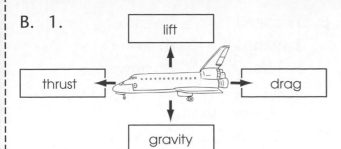

2. A: greater

B: greater

C: less

D: less

3. The forces of thrust and drag are unbalanced. The force of thrust is greater than the force of drag.

4. The object will either be lifting or dropping.

5. The forces of gravity and lift are balanced.

C. propels

1. propeller   2. jet engine

3. wings   4. wind

D. Check: A

1. drag   2. gravity

E. 1a.

b. Vehicle A has the least drag because it has the most streamlined shape and therefore the least air resistance.

c.

d. Parachutist A reaches the ground safely first because his parachute is small and has less air resistance and more speed than the other parachutes.

2.

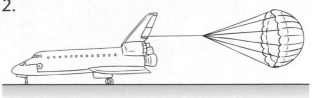

3   Flight: Moving Through Air

A. streamlined ; reducing

A, C, E

B. 1. rudder   2. elevators

3. ailerons

4a. Roll ; ailerons ; down

b. Yaw ; rudder

c. Pitch ; elevators ; up

5.

elevators — pitch motion
ailerons — roll motion
rudder — yaw motion

C. 1. engine and propeller
2. streamlined
3. weight
4. thrust

D. 1.

■ red ■ blue

Royal Canadian Air Force ;
3260 kilograms ; 1173 litres ;
180 – 590 km/h
11.12 metres ; 2.82 metres ;
9.75 metres

2a. pitching   b. yawing
c. rolling

Experiment

(Individual experiment outcome)

4 Bernoulli's Principle

A. 1. (Individual prediction)
(Suggested result)
The paper sank down between the books.
2. (Individual prediction)
(Suggested result)
The balloons moved closer to each other.

B. 1. speed   2. Faster
3. wings   4. lower
5. above   6. slower
7. lift   8. faster ; lower
9. slower ; higher

C. 1. Bernoulli's   2. airfoil
3. natural   4. lift
5. air   6. A, B, E

D. 1.

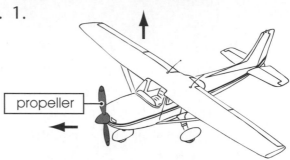

propeller

faster ; thrust ; lift

2.

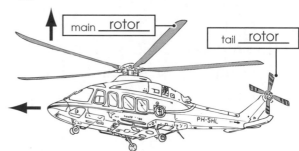

main rotor   tail rotor

lift ; thrust ; rotating

5 Living Things and Flight

A. 1. mate   2. food
3. prey   4. home
5. migrate   6. predators

B. B ; rotors
F ; float
A ; drag ; airfoil
I ; skin ; wing
C ; flap
D ; cycle
E ; thrust ; drag

ISBN: 978-1-897457-78-8

G ; propulsion
H ; flippers

C.

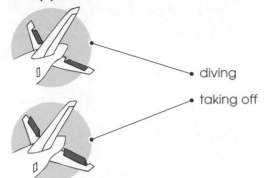

diving

taking off

Taking off   Gliding   Landing

D. 1. less than a penny ; 5.7 cm ; small ;
Cuba and the Caribbean
3.1 g ; 8.9 cm ; 10 cm ; North
America

2.

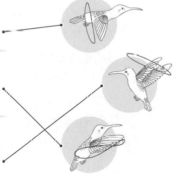

Flying forwards:
flapping its wings up and down like other birds

Hovering:
moving its wings rapidly back and forth in a figure-8 motion

Flying backwards:
the body is positioned vertically and the wings reach strongly back, down and up, making an oval in the air

6 Flight and Society

A. kites ; hot-air balloon ; glider ; Wright Brothers ; 1910 ; helicopter ; Russia ; moon

B. 1. A   2. C   3. B   4. A
5. (Suggested answers)
a. leisure/sightseeing
b. space exploration

C. (Suggested answers)
1: Benefits: The airport will promote tourism, which helps support the city economically and benefits the residents.
Costs: Schoolteachers may find the noise from planes disruptive to their teaching.
2: Benefits: Anglers will be able to travel more easily.
Costs: Travellers visiting the resort may find the noise from more frequent seaplanes disruptive.

D. 1. Airbus A380 ; allows people to travel anywhere fast ; infectious diseases can be spread globally
2. Sikorsky S-76 ; saves lives ; creates noise pollution in urban areas
3. Antonov An-2 ; makes fertilizing land fast and easy ; sprayed chemicals can harm nearby wild plants
4. Bombardier 415 ; locates and puts out fires ; uses an enormous amount of fuel

Experiment

(Possible experiment outcome)
Result: yes ; High pressure from the slow-moving air around the hair dryer's stream of low pressure air kept the ball in place.

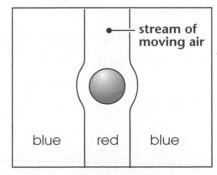

stream of moving air

blue   red   blue

fast ; low   slow ; high

Conclusion: Slow-moving air exerts more pressure than fast-moving air. ; supported

Review

A. 1. T   2. F   3. F   4. F

B. 1. (2)

2. (2)

3. (2)

4. (2)

5. (2)

circa 400 BCE; first flown in China

Italian inventor and artist

spinning propeller generates thrust

an airfoil shape in nature

air resistance allows it to fall slowly

C. 1. Air pushes on objects.

    Air can be compressed.

    Air resists things moving through it.

    Air takes up space.

    Air expands when heated.

    Air has an insulating property.

    Air has weight.

2a. No. An airplane needs air pressure to generate lift, but there is no air in space. Hence, airplanes cannot fly in space.

b. No. A kite needs wind to lift it up and be kept in the air. Since space has no air, kites cannot be flown in space.

D. 1.

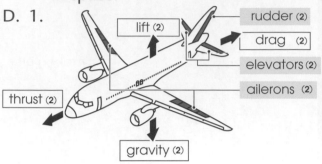

thrust (2) | lift (2) | rudder (2) | drag (2) | elevators (2) | ailerons (2) | gravity (2)

2a. It goes faster.

  b. It goes down.

  c. It goes slower.

3. The shape of an airplane's wing is an airfoil because it is curved. The shape takes advantage of Bernoulli's principle, which states that air flows faster over the top of the wing and slower underneath.

E. 1. (Suggested answers)

a. feathers create airfoil shape ; to catch prey

b. single wing rotors itself down and away from the parent tree ; to spread seeds for new trees to grow

2. (Suggested example)

A streamlined object reduces drag with its curved, smooth shape. A bicycle helmet is an example.

3. (Suggested answer)

Cost: Helicopters coming into the residential neighbourhood will create noise pollution and be disruptive to residents.

Benefit: It will be easier to transport people who live in remote areas to the hospital so they can be treated quickly.

Section 3

1 Current and Static Electricity

A. static ; A ; B ; contact
current ; C ; D ; flow

B. 1. equal   2. negative
3. positive
4.

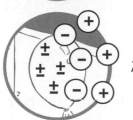

; = ; balloon

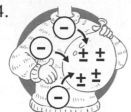

; <

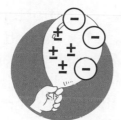

;

positive ; stick to the wall

C. D ; A ; C ; B

D. 1. power plants ; It is powerful and it does not run out. ; It is not portable and it can be dangerous. ; toasters ; ovens ; (Individual example)

2. batteries ; It is small and portable. ; It is not a very powerful energy source. ; cellphones ; flashlights ; (Individual example)

2 Simple Electrical Circuits

A. 1. electrons   2. battery
3. device   4. closed

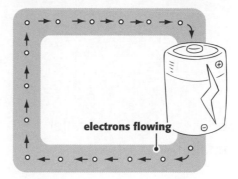

electrons flowing

5. positive   6. negative

B. 1. (Copy each symbol.)
2. closed   3. open
4. closed   5. closed
6. open   7. open

C.

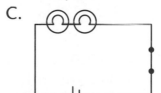

D.1a. dimmer   b. brighter
2.

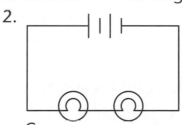

3 Parallel and Series Circuits

A. (Trace the dotted lines.)
1. Series ; one ; chain-like ; stop
2. Parallel ; branches ; keep

B. 1. parallel ; keeps
2. series ; stops
3. series ; stops
4. parallel ; keep

ISBN: 978-1-897457-78-8

Answers

C. (Suggested answers)

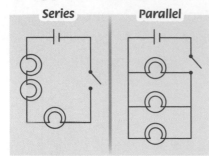

D. 1. series   2. parallel
   3. parallel   4. C, B, A

E.

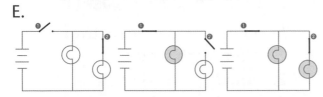

Experiment

(Suggested experiment outcome)
Result: The balloons repelled each other.
Conclusion: Two objects with like electrostatic charges repel each other. ; supported

4 Insulators and Conductors

A. (Suggested examples)
   1. insulator ; electrons ; pure water ; glass
   2. conductor ; allows ; tap water ; steel

B. 1a. insulator   b. conductor
    c. conductor   d. insulator
    They keep people safe from the electricity that flows through the conductors.

2. Circle: nail, paper clip, aluminum foil
    Electricity can flow through the nail, paper clip, and aluminum foil because they are conductors.

3. A, C, D
    Electricity can flow through rainwater, tap water, and mineral water because they contain metals and minerals that conduct electricity.

C. 1. roof   2. copper
   3. aluminum   4. lightning
   5. harmless   6. fire
   7. lightning rod   8. structure
   9. wire   10. ground
  11. They are conductors. They allow electricity from the lightning to flow through them to the ground.
  12. It is the CN Tower. It is 553.33 m tall.

5 Transformation of Energy

A.

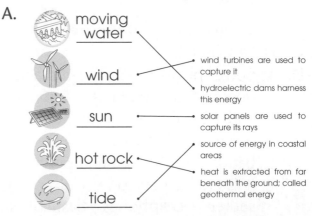

B. 1. battery   2. nuclear
   3. coal ; oil ; gas

ISBN: 978-1-897457-78-8

C. (Suggested answer)

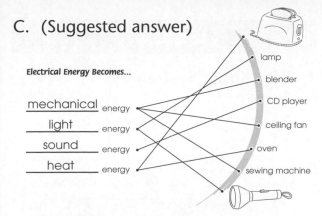

Electrical Energy Becomes...

mechanical energy
light energy
sound energy
heat energy

lamp
blender
CD player
ceiling fan
oven
sewing machine

D. 1. hydroelectric dam
   2. high-voltage power lines
   3. substation
   4. low-voltage power lines
   5. house
   6. electrical outlets

6 Electricity and Us

A. 1. land   2. toxic chemicals
   3. habitats   4. land
   5. air

B. 1. A   2. B
   3. A   4. renewable
   5. insulated   6. ceiling fans
   7. down   8. off
   9. (Suggested answer) Set computers to power-saving mode or turn them off when not in use.
   10. (Suggested answer) Use energy efficient appliances.

C. 1. Geothermal   2. heat
   3. underground   4. surface
   5. electricity   6. reach
   7. close   8. Iceland
   9. volcanoes   10. heats
   11. Hydroelectricity
   12. Yes, Iceland's electricity comes from geothermal energy and moving water, which are both renewable energy sources.

Experiment
(Individual experiment outcome)

Review
A. 1. F   2. T   3. F   4. T

B.

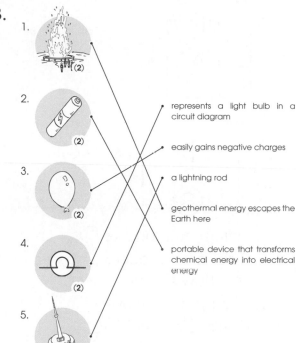

1.
2.
3.
4.
5.

represents a light bulb in a circuit diagram

easily gains negative charges

a lightning rod

geothermal energy escapes the Earth here

portable device that transforms chemical energy into electrical energy

C. (Suggested examples)
   1a. Current ; A flow of electric charge is transformed into heat, light, or mechanical energy. ; flashlight
   b. Static ; A stationary electric charge builds up on a material due to its contact with another material. ; plastic wrap

   2.

before rubbing   **after rubbing**

After rubbing, the electric charge that builds up on each strand of hair becomes the same and therefore

ISBN: 978-1-897457-78-8

the strands of hair start to repel each other.

D. 1.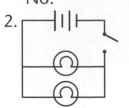

No.

2.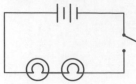

Yes.

3.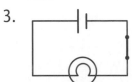

nail, metal fork, key

4. They are conductors, so electricity can flow through them.

E. 1. (Suggested answer)
Sources of Electricity
renewable: wind, moving water
non-renewable: fossil fuels, nuclear energy
Electrical Energy Can Become...
light ; lamp
heat ; oven

2. (Suggested examples)
Yes, smoke from power plants pollutes the air and hydroelectric dams wipe out habitats.

3. People build wind turbines that harness wind energy to generate electricity.

4. Anya should leave her lamp off and turn down the heat. If she is cold, she can wear warm pyjamas or use a thicker blanket.

Section 4

1 The Solar System

A. 1. axis   2. 1 day
   3. sun   4. orbit
   5. 365 days

B.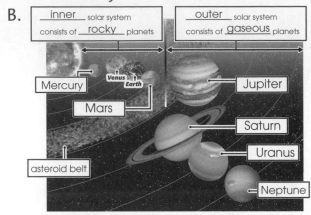

1. Venus   2. reddish

C. 1. meteoroid   2. meteor
   3. meteorite
   4. A meteoroid is a solid body smaller than an asteroid. It can be found in interplanetary space.
   5. A shooting star is a meteor, which burns with a bright streak through the atmosphere.
   6. (Individual answer)

2 Bodies in Motion

A. 1. satellite   2. sun   3. Earth
   4. 27 days   5. atmosphere ; craters

B.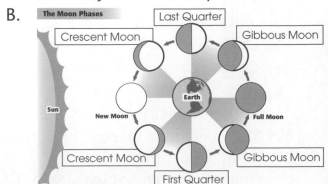

gibbous ; crescent

C. 1a. low tide   b. high tide
   2a. low tide   b. high tide

3 Lights in the Sky

A. 1. burning ; glows ; emit
   2. no ; reflects
   3. reflects light
   4. emits light

B. A: meteor ; emits
   B: moon ; reflects
   C: Milky Way ; emits
   D: constellation ; emits
   E: Jupiter ; reflects
   F: satellite ; reflects

C. 1. solar ; magnetic ; bright ; near the North Pole ; unpredictable ; after
   2. (Individual answer)

Experiment

(Individual experiment outcome)

4 Humans in Space

A. 1. 1961   2. Canadian
   3. female   4. 1999
   5. ISS   6. spacewalk

B. 1. food ; providing freeze-dried or dehydrated food that takes up less space
   2. air ; developing technology that makes air from water
   3. water ; recycling used water, including water vapour from exhaled air
   4. exercise ; providing machines and setting schedules for exercise

   5. hygiene ; providing personal urinal funnels with fans to suck air and waste into the commode

C. 1. Dennis Tito ; American ; engineer and multi-millionaire ; 2001 ; 7 days ; performed scientific experiments
   2. Guy Laliberté ; Canadian ; founder of Cirque du Soleil and the ONE DROP Foundation ; 2009 ; 11 days ; raise awareness for ONE DROP Foundation

5 Technology and Space

A. 1. E   2. C   3. A   4. D
   5. B

B. 1. Hubble Space Telescope ; universe
   2. planetarium ; constellations
   3. binoculars ; moon's surface
   4. telescope ; Saturn's rings

C. 1. B
   2. A solar eclipse is the blocking out of the sun's light when the moon passes between the Earth and the sun.
   3. It may cause eye damage or blindness.

6 Space Exploration and Society

A. Advantages: A, D, E
   Disadvantages: B, C

B. 1. astronomer ; celestial bodies
   2. astronaut ; pilot or crew member
   3. aerospace engineer ; satellites and spacecraft
   4. astrophysicist ; physical properties
   5. planetary geologist ; surface and interior processes

C. (Trace the dotted lines.)

1. communications: allows for telecommunications around the world

   navigation: provide positioning and navigation services

   weather: observe and monitor weather and climate, and predict weather conditions

2. (Individual answer)

Experiment

(Individual experiment outcome)

Review

A. 1. F   2. T   3. F   4. T

B.

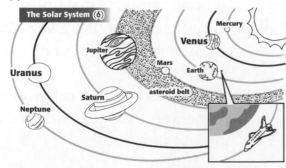

1.
2.
3.
4.
5.

the galaxy which contains our solar system

a group of stars that form a pattern as seen from the Earth

orbiting outside the Earth's atmosphere to take clear pictures of faraway galaxies

makes telecommunications around the world possible

a vehicle that explores the surface of a planet

C. 1.

The Solar System (6)

Mercury
Venus
Jupiter
Mars
Earth
Uranus
asteroid belt
Saturn
Neptune

2a. (Any two)
   Mercury, Venus, Earth, Mars

b. (Any two)
   Jupiter, Saturn, Uranus, Neptune

c. (Any two)
   Jupiter, Saturn, Uranus, Neptune

3. space shuttle

4. astronaut

5. (Suggested answer)
   Problem: no air in space
   Solution: developing technology that makes air from water

D. 1. Crescent Moon ; Full Moon ; Gibbous Moon ; Crescent Moon

2. a gibbous moon

3. about 27 days

4. No, it does not. We can see the moon because it reflects light from the sun.

5. (Suggested answer)
   binoculars

6. A solar eclipse and especially high tides occur.

E. 1. The Earth rotates on its axis in a counter-clockwise direction.

2. It is a space probe, which is an unmanned spacecraft.

3. (Suggested answer)
   An advantage is that it brings us new technology and a disadvantage is that it costs huge sums of money.

4. No, the moon has no atmosphere. It is covered with craters.

5. A lunar eclipse occurs when the Earth throws a dark shadow across the moon.

ISBN: 978-1-897457-78-8

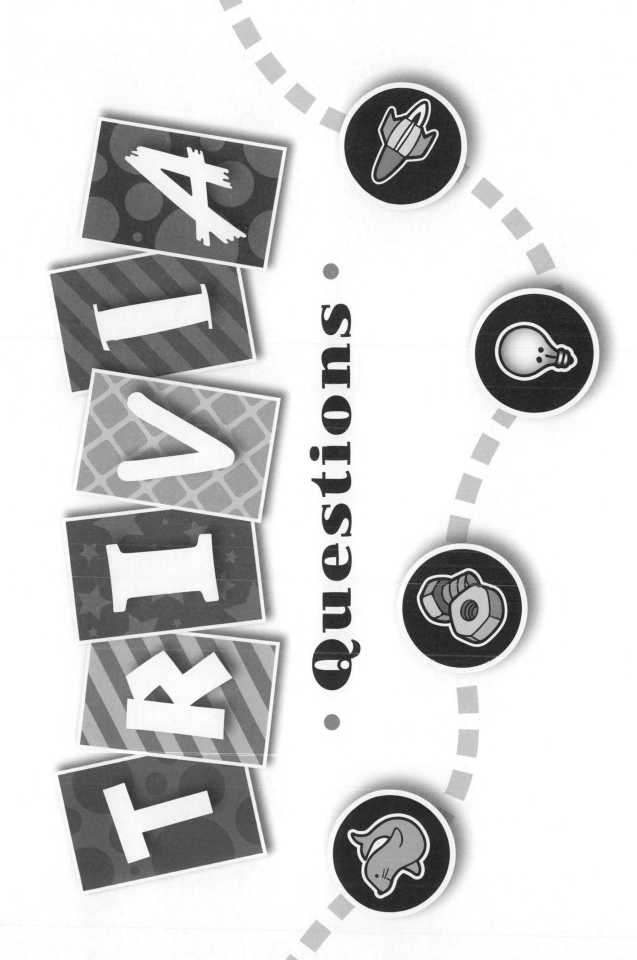

ISBN: 978-1-897457-78-8

ISBN: 978-1-897457-78-8

Can you break your funny bone?

True or False

The temperature at the centre of a beehive varies depending on the outside temperature.

What was the first song sung in space?

A. O Canada

B. Happy Birthday to You

C. Twinkle Twinkle Little Star

What is the largest biome in the world?

ISBN: 978-1-897457-78-8

Answer:

No, you cannot.

Your funny bone is not a bone at all, but a large nerve in your arm.

Answer:

false

The centre of a beehive stays between 33°C and 35°C, regardless of whether the outside temperature is 40°C or -40°C.

Answer:

B. Happy Birthday to You

It was sung in space by the crew of Apollo 9 on March 8, 1969.

Answer:

the ocean biome

The world's oceans make up 70% of the Earth's surface and are home to many species.

ISBN: 978-1-897457-78-8

True or False

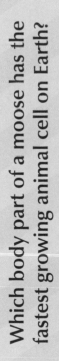

Great Bear Lake is the largest lake in the world.

True or False

Camels have three eyelids on each eye.

Which body part of a moose has the fastest growing animal cell on Earth?

A. its ears
B. its antlers
C. its legs
D. its teeth

How many kinds of minerals are there?

A. about 30
B. about 300
C. over 3000

ISBN: 978-1-897457-78-8

Answer:

false

Great Bear Lake is the largest lake in Canada, but not in the world. The largest lake in the world is the Caspian Sea, located near Russia and the eastern edges of Europe.

Answer:

B. its antlers

Answer:

true

Camels have an upper and lower eyelid like humans do, but they also have a third eyelid. This eyelid is very thin so that a camel can see clearly during sandstorms even with it closed.

Answer:

C. over 3000

Over 3000 kinds of minerals have been found so far and the list is still growing.

ISBN: 978-1-897457-78-8

How long does it take the Hubble Space Telescope to complete one revolution around the Earth?

A. 97 minutes

B. 24 hours

C. 365 days

True or False

Mount Rushmore is eroding at an alarming rate due to natural occurrences.

True or False

All bacteria are harmful to humans.

Beds are made from packed snow in Sweden's ice hotel. What are they topped with to provide extra comfort for its visitors?

A. tree branches and grass

B. spruce boughs and reindeer skins

C. sand and rocks

ISBN: 978-1-897457-78-8

Answer:

A. 97 minutes

Answer:

false

Some bacteria help us digest food, while others help us keep bad bacteria from getting into our bodies.

Answer:

false

The actual rate of erosion is only 2.5 cm over 10 000 years. This is because the mountain's rock is a smooth, fine-grained granite which is very durable.

Answer:

B. spruce boughs and reindeer skins

Spruce boughs act as an insulator to minimize the transfer of cold air to the visitor. Reindeer skins help trap the visitor's body heat.

ISBN: 978-1-897457-78-8

What do predators consider a skunk's black and white colouring to be?

A. a camouflage

B. a warning

C. a greeting

Which three metals make up the centre part of a toonie?

The first car did not have steering wheels. What did drivers use to steer instead?

A. lever

B. wedge

C. screwdriver

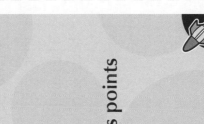

The tail of a comet always points away from the sun.

ISBN: 978-1-897457-78-8

Answer:

B. a warning

A skunk's distinctive pattern and bold colouring lets potential predators know that they should not get too close.

Answer:

copper, aluminum, and nickel

The centre of a toonie is made up of 92% copper, 6% aluminum, and 2% nickel.

Answer:

A. lever

Steering wheels were not widely used until the early 1900s.

Answer:

true

The tail always points away from the sun because of solar wind.

  ISBN: 978-1-897457-78-8

Venus has the longest days out of any planet in our solar system. How many Earth days are in one Venus day?

A. 7 days
B. 31 days
C. 243 days
D. 315 days

True or False

Dew forms on grass in the morning because grass sweats like humans during the night.

True or False

The CN Tower is made of very strong materials so it never sways even in strong winds.

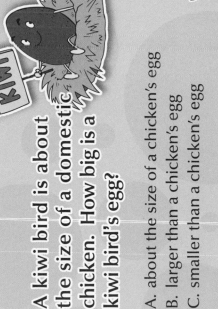

A kiwi bird is about the size of a domestic chicken. How big is a kiwi bird's egg?

A. about the size of a chicken's egg
B. larger than a chicken's egg
C. smaller than a chicken's egg

ISBN: 978-1-897457-78-8

Answer:

C. 243 days

Answer:

false

The top of the CN Tower can sway as much as 1 metre from its centre on windy days. If it did not sway, the tower would get pushed over or snap.

Answer:

false

Dew forms on grass because moisture in the air condenses in the colder temperatures of the early morning.

Answer:

B. larger than a chicken's egg

A kiwi bird's egg is up to six times the size of a chicken's egg.

ISBN: 978-1-897457-78-8

On which planet will you be the heaviest?

A. Jupiter

B. Venus

C. Mercury

D. Mars

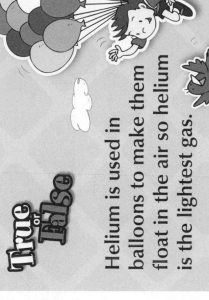

True or False

Helium is used in balloons to make them float in the air so helium is the lightest gas.

Where can you find the biggest house in the world?

A. China

B. the United States

C. England

D. Canada

Can an owl move its head in a full circle?

ISBN: 978-1-897457-78-8

Answer:

A. Jupiter

Your weight on Jupiter is about 2.4 times your weight on Earth.

Answer:

C. England

The Windsor Castle in England is the biggest house in the world. It is one of the residences of Queen Elizabeth II.

Answer:

false

Helium is the second-lightest gas. The lightest gas is hydrogen, but since it is highly flammable, it is not used in balloons.

Answer:

No, it cannot.

An owl can move its head 270°. Since an owl cannot move its eyes within its sockets like humans can, it must move its entire head to see what is around it.

ISBN: 978-1-897457-78-8

Almost all birds have nostrils at the tops of their beaks. But there is one species whose nostrils are at the end of its beak. Which one is it?

A. kiwi bird
B. bald eagle
C. barn owl
D. ostrich

 True or False

Magnets can attract anything that is made of metal.

What are Saturn's rings made up of?

A. steam
B. ice and rocks
C. gas and metals

Which planet has the biggest moon in the solar system?

A. Earth
B. Mars
C. Jupiter

ISBN: 978-1-897457-78-8

Answer:

A. kiwi bird

The position of a kiwi bird's nostrils allows the kiwi bird to easily smell prey that is underground or close to the ground, such as worms and small insects.

Answer:

false

Aluminum is non-magnetic. This is why you cannot attract a piece of aluminum foil to a refrigerator magnet.

Answer:

B. ice and rocks

They are made up of mostly ice particles and some rock particles ranging in size from a centimetre to ten metres.

Answer:

C. Jupiter

This moon is called Ganymede. It is even larger than Mercury.

ISBN: 978-1-897457-78-8

True or False

All spiders weave webs.

How many moons are there in the solar system?

A. 1
B. 64
C. 128
D. 169

About how fast does a rocket need to travel to overcome the Earth's gravity?

A. 41 000 km/h
B. 10 000 km/h
C. 2900 km/h
D. 1000 km/h

True or False

The densest element on Earth is a metal.

ISBN: 978-1-897457-78-8

Answer:

false

Some spiders, such as the Goliath Bird-eater spider, do not weave webs.

Answer:

D. 169

Answer:

A. 41 000 km/h

At that speed, you could travel from Toronto to Vancouver in 5 minutes!

Answer:

true

The densest element is osmium. Its density is about 1.2 times that of gold.

ISBN: 978-1-897457-78-8

True or False

The height of the Great Pyramid of Giza has stayed the same since it was built 4500 years ago.

True or False

All penguins live in the Antarctic.

Not all animals have pink tongues. Which of these animals has a blue tongue?

A. big-horned sheep

B. polar bear

C. tiger

D. bison

If the sun suddenly stopped shining, how long would it take us to realize it?

A. right away

B. about 10 seconds

C. about 8 minutes

D. about an hour

ISBN: 978-1-897457-78-8

Answer:

false

Its height has decreased 7 metres due to erosion.

Answer:

B. polar bear

A polar bear's tongue is blue, which is the colour of its skin underneath its fur.

Answer:

false

Only a few species of penguins live in the Antarctic. Many of them live in warmer places in the Southern Hemisphere and some even live close to the equator.

Answer:

B. about 8 minutes

It takes about 8 minutes for sunlight to reach the Earth.

ISBN: 978-1-897457-78-8

How many dimples are there on a golf ball?

A. 100 to 199

B. 200 to 249

C. 250 to 450

D. 451 to 800

Spider silk is stronger than steel of the same diameter.

All deserts are hot.

The word "rodent" comes from the Latin word "rodere". What does "rodere" mean?

A. small mammal

B. long tail

C. to gnaw

D. to dig

Answer:

C. 250 to 450

The dimples on a golf ball allow it to travel farther.

Answer:

true

Spider silk is five times stronger than steel.

Answer:

false

Deserts are defined by their lack of precipitation, not their temperature. In fact, the entire continent of Antarctica is considered a desert.

Answer:

C. to gnaw

Rodents have front upper and lower teeth that grow continuously, so they must keep their teeth short by gnawing.

ISBN: 978-1-897457-78-8

True or False

Porcupines throw their quills.

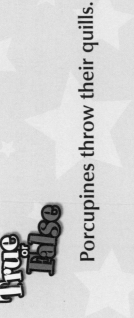

Of all the water in the world, how much water is drinkable?

A. less than 1%
B. about 30%
C. about 70%

The constellation Orion (The Hunter) has a "belt". How many bright stars make up this "belt"?

A. 1
B. 3
C. 10

What does a firefly need to stimulate the chemical reaction in its body that gives off light?

A. water
B. oxygen
C. carbon dioxide
D. electricity

Answer:

false

Porcupines cannot throw their quills, but their quills are easily detached from their bodies so that they stick onto predators.

Answer:

A. less than 1%

97% of the world's water is saline (salty) water, which is not drinkable. Drinkable water comes from rivers, freshwater lakes, and from underground.

Answer:

B. 3

Answer:

B. oxygen

ISBN: 978-1-897457-78-8

What would happen if there was no atmosphere on Earth?

A. The air would be fresher.

B. There will be more meteorite hits.

C. There would not be any living things on Earth.

What is a cloud forest?

A. a large group of clouds in the sky

B. a cloud that looks like a forest

C. a forest often blanketed by low cloud cover

D. a forest on a mountain

True or False

Salt makes ice melt faster and sugar makes it melt slower.

True or False

Sunlight cannot reach very deep into the ocean, so there is no light there.

ISBN: 978-1-897457-78-8

Answer:

C. There would not be any living things on Earth.

The Earth's atmosphere helps maintain a favourable temperature for living things. Without the atmosphere, no living thing can survive.

Answer:

C. a forest often blanketed by low cloud cover

Answer:

false

Both salt and sugar can lower the melting point of ice and make ice melt faster.

Answer:

false

Although it is true that sunlight cannot reach the depths of the ocean, many deep ocean creatures, like the deep sea anglerfish, produce their own light to attract prey.

ISBN: 978-1-897457-78-8